MENTAL TOUGHNESS FOR ATHLETES: THE PROVEN PATH TO PEAK PERFORMANCE

HOW PROFESSIONAL ATHLETES TRAIN THEIR MINDS TO WIN THE GAME BEFORE IT BEGINS

JJ MILLION

© Copyright 2022 - All rights reserved.

The content contained within this book may not be reproduced, duplicated or transmitted without direct written permission from the author or the publisher.

Under no circumstances will any blame or legal responsibility be held against the publisher, or author, for any damages, reparation, or monetary loss due to the information contained within this book, either directly or indirectly.

Legal Notice:

This book is copyright protected. It is only for personal use. You cannot amend, distribute, sell, use, quote or paraphrase any part, or the content within this book, without the consent of the author or publisher.

Disclaimer Notice:

Please note the information contained within this document is for educational and entertainment purposes only. All effort has been executed to present accurate, up to date, reliable, complete information. No warranties of any kind are declared or implied. Readers acknowledge that the author is not engaged in the rendering of legal, financial, medical or professional advice. The content within this book has been derived from various sources. Please consult a licensed professional before attempting any techniques outlined in this book.

By reading this document, the reader agrees that under no circumstances is the author responsible for any losses, direct or indirect, that are incurred as a result of the use of the information contained within this document, including, but not limited to, errors, omissions, or inaccuracies.

TO MY KIDS — YOU CAN BE AND DO ANYTHING YOU DESIRE, ALL YOU HAVE TO DO IS *START*.

— DAD

CONTENTS

Introduction	ix
1. IT'S ALL IN YOUR HEAD	1
Let's Define Mindset	3
Why Is Your Mindset so Important?	6
Self-esteem	6
Perspective	7
Seize the Momentum	8
Face Adversity	8
Achieve the Goal	9
Flexible Mindset in Sports	10
The Psychology of Motivation	14
Instinctive Motivation Theory	15
Driving Theory	16
Arousal Theory	17
Humanistic Theory	17
Expectancy Theory	21
How to Develop a Winning Mindset	21
Being Talented Doesn't Make You Successful	23
Start With Small Steps	24
Strengthen Your Character	25
Trust Your Vision, Trust Your Instincts	26
Take Action	27
INTERACTIVE EXERCISES	27
2. WHERE THE MIND GOES, THE BODY FOLLOWS	30
The Power of Visualization	32
How It Enhances Sports Performance	36
Building Mental Strength	38
Five Tips to Visualize Like an Olympian Athlete	40
Know What You Want	41
Keep It Specific	41

Use Images	42
Don't Forget to Practice	42
Combine Visualization With Training	42
INTERACTIVE EXERCISES	43
3. DEALING WITH SPORTS ANXIETY	**46**
Sports Anxiety	50
What Is It?	50
Causes	51
What Increases the Risk of Suffering It?	52
Anxiety vs Excitement: What's the Difference?	54
Relabeling Anxiety as Excitement	56
Coping With Sports Performance Anxiety	60
INTERACTIVE EXERCISES	61
4. SELF-BELIEF AND RESILIENCE	**66**
The Complex Art of Believing in Yourself	69
The Athlete's Worst Fears	71
Let's Define Resilience	73
How Resilience Impact Sports?	74
INTERACTIVE EXERCISES	75
5. BECOMING EMOTIONALLY INTELLIGENT	**79**
Emotional Intelligence: an Overview	79
Emotional Intelligence in Sports	80
Enhance Your Emotions, Enhance Your Performance	82
INTERACTIVE EXERCISES	85
6. YOUR CHANCE TO INSPIRE SOMEONE ELSE	**88**
7. TOUGH LIKE STEEL	**90**
Mental Toughness in Athletes	90
Its Importance in Sports	91
INTERACTIVE EXERCISES	93
8. DEALING WITH YOUR FEARS	**95**
Fear of Failure	95
What Is It?	96
Symptoms	96

How to Overcome It?	98
Fear of Missing Out	99
INTERACTIVE EXERCISES	102
9. COMMON MISTAKES ATHLETES MAKE	105
Newbies Blunders	107
Veteran Blunders	108
Afterword	111
10. TIME TO PASS THE BATON	115
Bibliography	117

INTRODUCTION

Impossible is just a big word thrown around by small men who find it easier to live in the world they've been given than to explore the power they have to change it. Impossible is not a fact. It's an opinion. Impossible is not a declaration. It's a dare. Impossible is potential. Impossible is temporary. Impossible is nothing.

—Muhammad Ali

My running history began before my marriage when I was 30 years old. Like any man with a paunch, I wanted to be skinny at the wedding. I asked my tailor to make me a suit two sizes too small, and I decided to try to get into it.

Like any amateur athlete, the beginning was hard, especially with my way of being and the mindset I carried with me then. At first, I was my worst enemy. Undermining my chances of success by setting unrealistic goals and disappointing myself when (logically) I did not meet them.

Introduction

A 30-year-old man who starts in this discipline must first learn to walk before running. Retrace the path progressively with realistic, concrete, and, above all, short-term goals. Would I like to run the New York Marathon? Yes. But I couldn't do it. Not yet.

The wedding was six months away, and I was confident that a little physical activity and caring about my meals would be enough to meet my expectations.

I found a park near my house and started walking.

The circuit stretched, from start to finish, over three miles. It seemed like a reasonable distance, which took me about an hour to complete at a man's pace. Without knowing it, a significant change in my life began to take shape.

At first, I went twice a week, and walking the entire circuit took me about an hour. Then, when I knew little, I added another day of training. This is how the first months passed, which are usually very positive. In my case, at least, that enemy rarely attacked me at the beginning of the change.

If it happened to me, and I clearly noticed it, that sometimes I lowered the time I covered those three miles a little and was filled with enthusiasm. But as soon as that time went up again, for whatever reason, I was invaded by a profound disappointment.

Until that moment, I had practiced countless sports throughout my entire life. Judo as a mid-school kid. Then, in high school, I dedicated myself to playing soccer, only to discover my own limitations with the practice of this game.

Introduction

The same thing happened to me with basketball, gym, and weightlifting routines.

Every time I felt that I was making some progress, I would lose momentum, desire, and enthusiasm if it was not sustained over time. All that enthusiasm, that motivation, that desire to improve myself disappeared from one day to another.

Going for a run changed some bad mental habits in my life; however, I still don't know if running was the discipline that changed me... Or if I had already changed without realizing it when I started.

The routine was more or less the same. I would go and run the same course, over and over, every week. The exact distance at the same time (give it or take a few seconds). Until one specific night, there was one life-changing moment for me.

I was running with a friend, and we came to a split. The circuit continued to our right, undertaking those three miles last section. For months, we had done this without any route changes or modifications. So I tried turning right that night, but my friend went straight.

He totally ignored the course and extended it without consulting me. I had never run more than three miles in my life. It was my limit, my magic number. Not only had I never done it, but the possibility of achieving it, of overcoming that distance, never crossed my mind.

My friend looked at me as he avoided that curve, as if inviting me to follow his lead. I perfectly remember my reaction of instant disbelief and insecurity. I step out of my

Introduction

comfort zone, out of the path I knew like the back of my hands. I knew its sidewalk holes, loose tiles, and those that rose due to the trees' roots' sprouting.

We circled this turnoff and returned to the original path, further down the road. When we finished the race, the final distance marked 1.25 more miles on the clock. I had exceeded a self-imposed limit for the first time in my life.

My friend's diversion, something as simple as that, was an epiphany for me. A revealed truth that he irrefutably proved to me that he could give more. That no one knew my limits, not even me.

From that moment on, I let go. My head changed. I was running differently, feeling better. I took off a heavy backpack and gained confidence. It was the first time in my life that I felt truly capable of something new. It was the first time I felt complete.

It didn't take a month for me to break that personal record again. The second time, I was alone. I no longer needed my friend to extend his hand and invite me to improve myself. I understood that I could do it without help. And so began a path of self-improvement, which I will tell you about as we see the different themes of this book.

We will learn essential concepts of sports psychology, and we will go step by step proposing superior strategies so that you can meet your goals.

If you are reading this, it is most likely that you are engaged in the practice of some sport, and you want to be better at it. Leaving life in each moment, surrendering entirely, and embracing the results: whether they are good or bad.

If you are reading this, you have had moments like the one I told you about, where the great adversary to overcome is oneself.

Regardless of the sport you practice, whether individual or team, our mental disposition to the field of play is essential. The right mindset can build entire careers, successful athletes, and exceptional sporting achievements.

On the contrary, a poor mindset when practicing any sports discipline will (without a doubt) be detrimental. This is a scientifically proven fact and repeated ad nauseam by world-class athletes and athletes, stars in their respective sports. For your goals, for your spirit, and for your mental health.

We will see different ways for our minds to be one with us throughout this writing. We will face our fears and insecurities with the firm conviction that they are necessary. They add value to our victories and teach us about our defeats, but in no way should they be the drivers of the ship.

Our fears and insecurities will be accessories. Satellites of the major plan.

I invite you to return to the words that begin this brief introduction. Read the quote, analyze every word. Every concept. It is beautiful. Right?

Think of the impossible as an invention of those who lack the courage to transcend. Small men and women, controlled by fear, stand in that comfortable position,

Introduction

believing they cannot be overcome. They don't have the power.

Think of the word impossible as an opinion, not as a fact. As something totally relative and personal. Own of each human being. There will be those who feel it is like a fact, failing to break the barrier of fear.

Meanwhile, those who handle the impossible as an opinion will be able to give it the entity that corresponds to it and follow their paths as their hearts dictate.

Consider the concept of the impossible as a challenge to achieve it. As a potential market for teachings, morals, and new challenges. Like a temporary idea, like a fantasy that disappears when it is fulfilled.

And that invites us to contemplate that nothing is impossible if our mind, body, and heart are aligned with our goals. It must be a sincere alignment that grows from the depths of our being and transforms us structurally.

Do you feel it? Do you perceive it? Let's go for it!

1

IT'S ALL IN YOUR HEAD

What do you think if I mention the name of George Clooney? Surely the first image that comes to mind is that of a successful Hollywood actor. Talented, lovely, charismatic, even a millionaire. An example to be followed by those who want to succeed in their respective activities.

This image that Clooney projects is only a part of his life. A portion of his history and the experiences that he lived through. It is the final part that figures him as an already consecrated man. I will not deny that it serves as a source of inspiration, as a beacon that motivates his drive to succeed.

However, his success is only part of his story. Only a partial clipping of his life tells us there must be something behind it. At a moment in time, he declared himself to be the cornerstone of the beginning of his career. Clooney was not born successful, talented, or a millionaire.

Before even considering becoming an actor, George

dreamed of being a baseball player, like most kids in his native Kentucky. He used to go to the Great American Ball Park (home of the Cincinnati Reds) with his friends, and together they would enter the stadium to watch the games.

There, with the view of the Ohio River drawing the landscape in the background, Clooney tried to become a baseball player, taking the trials to join the Red's professional baseball team. At the time, he was 16 years old and faced stronger, more talented, and experienced young adults in his trials, who beat him hands down. This represented a strong shock for him and his family. They were all convinced that his path in life would be to become a professional baseball player. However, he didn't make the cut.

At 18, Clooney found himself reconsidering his entire life. He went through two universities to study journalism and failed to graduate. Finally, he understood that he had to start working. What to do from that moment on if destiny had already rejected your greatest wish?

Throughout those years, between 18 and 21, Clooney had several jobs. He worked as a waiter and a street vendor. For a while, he sold women's shoes and men's suits. He even worked for a few months as a bricklayer. All this without seriously considering dedicating himself to acting.

When he understood that he wanted to be an actor, he spent years struggling to get an opportunity. They were painful years in which he faced (like the vast majority of actors) the almost constant rejection of the audition market.

When he got tired of the negativity of the business, and he understood that, if he kept doing the same thing, the results would not change, he took control of the situation. He decided to call other larger agencies, posing as a representative. Once he contacted them, he started selling himself. He told the other agents about this guy, a new talent looking to work in the business. Some guy named Clooney. Let them notice him. He did not get a job this way, but got a lot of auditions.

He decided to stop complaining about the opportunities that didn't come up and took matters into his own hands.

There were so many negative responses that he learned to value them. To live with them and to become strong through rejection. His first big break would come in 1984, at the age of 23. His first gig was ER. The rest is history.

Let's Define Mindset

We can define mindset as the set of thoughts, beliefs, and attitudes that determine how a person lives their life. If the human brain is a computer, the mindset is the operating system that controls it.

It determines our ideas, how we act and perceive the results of our actions, and how we deal with the consequences of our behavior. Taken to the basics, mindset is the mentality with which we move through life.

Thanks to the studies carried out by Dr. Carol Dweck (psychologist and professor at Stanford University) in the field of motivation and the development of personalities in elementary school youth, can be separated into two types of mentalities or mindsets: one fixed and one of growth.

The fixed mindset occurs when people think that talent is innate and that intelligence as quality is enough to be successful in life. In this way, they consider that human grades are fixed traits and, therefore, cannot be changed, lost, nor acquired.

According to Dweck, in a fixed mindset, they spend the time of their lives documenting their intelligence rather than developing it. They believe that through talent, one can survive effortlessly.

These types of people tend to worry about appearing intelligent to others, with an attitude that is not very receptive to criticism (even if it is constructive). They feel diminished when people in close circles achieve their goals, exhibit suspicious behavior, and show clear signs of insecurity.

Despite knowing (or believing) themselves to be intelligent, that feeling of internal insecurity in their hearts keeps them from taking on new challenges. They constantly avoid challenges, and if they manage to get out of their comfort zone, they usually abandon the idea at the first obstacle.

They are people who seek perfection, convinced that it is a definite possibility, without understanding that it is a concept as abstract as it is impossible. Nobody will ever be perfect.

On the contrary, those with a growth mindset are committed to exceeding their goals and fulfilling their objectives through effort and dedication. They have a mentality that means putting the will above all else as an essential act to satisfy their desires and fulfill their ambitions.

These people conceive the skill set as a dynamic, constantly changing, and moving set of talents. They believe that they can improve any of their abilities through effort and practice. They face their goals without excuses and constantly walk the path that brings them closer to them.

We will see, throughout the book, how this mentality keeps appearing. That's because it's the one that we all want to incorporate into our lives, and the one shared by a large part of high-level athletes.

They are those who understand learning as a process that takes time, effort, and sacrifice. They consider that the error is an intrinsic part related to the art of learning and improving. They know that through them, they will be able to enrich their experience.

For this reason, they are also people who accept the challenges that life presents and challenge themselves as well. They go out of their comfort zone to learn new things, being inspired by the success of others. They are also receptive and appreciate constructive criticism, which they consider part of the learning process described above.

The truth is that we are all a mix of fixed and growth mindsets. Perhaps in some areas of our lives, we are more open to the idea of growth, more receptive, and bolder. While in other aspects or moments, the features of the fixed mindset are present. It will be essential to cope with these moments, recognize what triggers the fixed mindset, understand it, and act on it.

Why Is Your Mindset so Important?

The mindset with which one approaches each minute is critical to success. It is an essential factor that influences (directly or indirectly) all aspects of life, personal and professional. Therefore, it will be crucial to understand which mentality is positive for us and which is not.

That decision will have to do with our character and personality. Incorporating a flexible mentality into our lives will be a crucial ingredient for the correct progress on the projects we decide to undertake.

The right mindset is a big difference between those who thrive in life and those who don't. It will be the first variable to consider when undertaking projects, setting goals and aiming for success.

If you have an idea, and you want to consolidate it or put it into practice, you must master that mindset. Make it part of your life. Next, we will see different areas where a good mentality directly influences.

Self-esteem

The correct programming of your mindset will have instant positive effects on your mind and your heart. The first, the one that becomes evident almost automatically, is the improvement of self-esteem.

A flexible mindset with good self-esteem will allow you to consider yourself capable of achieving any goal you set for yourself. Your mind focuses on what you need to meet your goals and puts aside the opinions of others. It has to do with how we perceive ourselves, how we put our value to the test, and what we say to ourselves in that internal talk that builds the integral vision of our being.

We all have an opinion formed about ourselves. I analyzed what I would think of myself more than once if I were a third party. Suppose I could change my perspective and see myself from the outside. In my case, depending on the day and mood, the answer may vary. But not so much. Always within healthy margins.

In general, healthy self-esteem and a positive mindset are two sides of the same coin. They are two correlative aspects between them. In this case, the attitude must be conceived as a tool. We have a resource to pave the way that directs us to our projects and dreams.

We must understand that we are responsible for ourselves, our minds and how we put together our set of behaviors through it.

Remember that we are not what we say, but what we do.

Perspective

Perspective is an essential part of how we perceive ourselves. It is a valuable quality to build a firm path to success. It has to do with how we read the things that happen to us in life and their effect on our minds. The correct perspective can help de-dramatize difficult situations and make them less important. However, it must be used responsibly and nurtured with a positive mindset.

It will be decisive to process the information and experiences of our daily lives in a healthy and orderly way. Learn to play intelligently with the cards dealt to us by the world around us. Building an optimistic mindset increases the chances of succeeding in what we set out to do, formulating a positive perspective to face long-term projects.

Seize the Momentum

When we define an important goal for our lives, the first big step is to move towards it. That determination that one adopts to meet their goals includes the process of committing in a sustained manner through the art of exercising will and effort. It is through momentum that progress is made. And although it is natural that, at times, the motivation declines and some structures tremble, if one is clear about the objective and the impulse is sufficient, then the probability of success will be greater.

Driving that impulse correctly, and channeling it positively to focus efforts and reinforce commitment, is key to success. Well-directed momentum will allow you to maintain motivation and sustain effort over time.

Face Adversity

Adversities are an inherent part of the human process. Every path and goal you set for yourself will come with its share of difficulties, and adopting a positive mindset is essential to overcome them.

For flexible mindsets, overcoming those difficult moments will be synonymous with teaching. The one who sees the glass half full, and can positively interpret the events and happenings that are presented to him, will have greater possibilities of sustaining the effort and fulfilling his objectives.

It is clear that when something fails, feelings of negativity arise. Those who are softer from mental issues will feel the need to throw in the towel, drop, and leave the race. However, optimists will see it differently. For them, adversities are unique and unrepeatable moments that enrich the learning experience.

Thanks to a positive mindset, you will be able to assimilate the blow, feel it and suffer it (because, in the end, we are human beings) and continue on your way. With the toughness of having been hardened, the renewed conviction and the corresponding teaching to face the challenges. Head held high and step still sure.

Achieve the Goal

As we have seen, setting goals is a process that involves many variables. To begin with, define the idea with the necessary security to know that it is indeed what we want to achieve. Then, the impulse and decision-making activate the march on the previously outlined path. That march is obtained through security and personal motivation.

Once you begin to retrace your path towards your goal, you must have the will to sustain the effort over time and the courage to overcome adversity. You must arm yourself with your strengths, make a foothold in those aspects of your life that are best for you, and make an effort.

Build a proper mindset that allows you to get through bad times and not lose the inertia you've acquired up to that point.

You must exercise your courage, know the sacrifices ahead, and overcome the hurdles until the moment of success—the moment of achievement.

From that moment, when you reach your goal, you can feel satisfied that you have achieved it. This is the indicator, the end of the journey. Later, times of thoughtful analysis will come.

Thus begins a period in which, with the objective in his pocket, you will be able to seriously analyze the path you have traveled, your virtues and defects, your successes and mistakes. You will be able to balance the cost and benefit of said goal, what the experience generated internally, and what teaching it has left you.

If you consider yourself ready to embark on your path and have these steps in mind, then incorporate a positive attitude and do it.

Flexible Mindset in Sports

If an athlete came to stand out above the rest, in whatever discipline, that rise not only had to do with his talent and innate qualities, but a large part of that process is mental. Most high-performance athletes have a flexible mindset, allowing constant growth and learning. They are professionals who fully understand their capabilities, limitations, and their respective activities' realistic goals.

They are perfectionists, detail-oriented, and meticulous in their training. They serve as an inspiration to their teammates. They invite them to improve themselves and maximize their potential, which will be contagious if they have a positive attitude. They are usually the first to arrive and the last to leave each practice.

As we mentioned before, no matter the sport, whether it is individual or in a team, an athlete who stands out is an athlete who maintains a positive mentality. This way of seeing things, applied to training and optimizing their results within the discipline they practice, helps them obtain a clear advantage over others.

They are athletes in total control of their emotions. They know that through this control, having their joys and sorrows under their radar, they will be able to generate positive changes in their body, life, and sports performance.

Of course, there will be difficult times, even for the most successful athletes. High-performance competitors must deal with an injury, a drop in performance, your coach's pressure, and the public's expectations. In these cases, staying positive is a challenge.

We will see some concrete strategies to beat the negativity and adopt a mindset that removes self-imposed limits.

When those difficult moments are present, frustration attacks, or pessimism sets in, it is essential to understand that the first thing to do is change your mood. Focus on the positive issues without getting encapsulated in the depressing reasons you or that affect your performance.

When one sets an objective, whatever it may be, the path to the goal is hardly impeccable, unpolluted, and devoid of challenges, failures, or adversities. As we already mentioned, obstacles are part of the path. It is necessary to learn from them and take them as a natural part.

However, one thing does not remove the other. As much as one has a positive, flexible, and growth mindset, obstacles affect us. There's no way to escape.

We can raise our spirits, and for this, the options are varied and will be very personal. Some people listen to music or hang out with friends. They support their sorrows there and try to change their state of mind.

Others spend part of their time in hobbies, taking long soaking baths, reading a book, or playing with their children. Whatever works for you, whatever changes your mentality, brings you back to the positive zone, brings a smile to your face, will be valid and necessary to overcome obstacles.

Another option is to take a break. This is not usually the first choice for athletes. Rarely do they decide to stop for a moment, recover energy and continue. They tend to believe that the act of braking is counterproductive and that resting is wasting time. For them, slowing down and taking a break is allowing their competitors to improve, which is inadmissible.

However, it is essential to know your time to be able to rest without losing ground to the competition. You can stop for a moment, rethink things and come back refreshed. Sometimes a step back is valid if it means taking two steps forward.

Another productive strategy for overcoming obstacles and staying positive along the way is the self-talk exercise. Various psychological studies have shown that maintaining a constant internal dialogue improves performance in different sports disciplines. This link with the increase in performance has to do with what is said and believed. A mindset in which you start to believe what you tell yourself. And therefore, you can achieve what you believe.

Some athletes repeat mantras. Others, mentalize from concentration or visualize their family and friends. They take positive things from their lives and incorporate them into the dynamics of the sport they practice, to relax and improve their spirits.

Scientists focus their studies on measuring athletes' anxiety levels and how they feel about their confidence, efficiency, and performance levels. These conversations with oneself involve self-knowledge, retracing a path of personal and professional development, and it is a positive long-term strategy. It must be incorporated as a habit, as something recurring daily.

The idea of positive visualization is to imagine that you are competing, winning, and doing well. Give it as much detail as possible, and trust that if you can imagine it, you can do it. Generate positive expectations about what may happen, and do everything possible to meet them. Visualization exercises, for example, are positive strategies to reduce stress and get in the right mindset for the sport you play.

The first time I ran a half-marathon, I remember having difficulty falling asleep the night before. My mind was moving at a thousand miles an hour. Every time I closed my eyes, I imagined the entire route. I thought about how I would physically get to that point in the race. I visualized myself crossing the finish line and fulfilling that goal.

When I managed to fall asleep and have a good night's rest the next day for the race, I was already mentally prepared to undertake that project. That previous visualization helped me to relax and gain confidence.

In short, attitude is fundamental to the sport. It does not matter the discipline, the type of sport, or the level you practice.

Whether a high achiever or an amateur, having your mind aligned with the goal and staying positive will give you the tools to improve yourself, meet your goals, and live up to your expectations.

Try any of these strategies, and trust your ability and your performance. A flexible mindset is the right set of thoughts and behaviors to do this.

The Psychology of Motivation

Motivation explains why people start, sustain, and finish a behavior for a given time. It is part of the emphasis that the person has to fulfill a goal or satisfy a need. The creation, impulse, and implementation of the actions the subject believes are necessary to reach the previously set goal will depend on the motivation.

It is a personal, internal state that activates, directs, and maintains certain behaviors. Motivational states have different degrees and strengths, depending on how much motivation influences the person's behavior and behaviors.

Although humans and animals can apply motivation, the difference is that the human being acts for reasons and is committed to their actions, analyzing the results and sustaining (if necessary) the behaviors. On the other hand, animals act instinctively, following their desires.

Thanks to motivation, man advances on their goals. They make decisions, direct their energy, and maintain their behaviors. The forces behind motivation can be biological, social, cognitive, or emotional. We will see the different theories that encompass this concept. Let's do it!

Instinctive Motivation Theory

This theory contemplates that the behaviors of human beings are motivated by evolutionary aspects. Fear, love, modesty, and shame are some factors (specific to survival) that encourage man to take certain behaviors and sustain them over time.

However, this postulate doesn't consider man's learning along the way to the goal and how the initial motivations could transform. It assumes that man acts impulsively and does not fully explain the behavior, but only describes it.

This theory has lost ground over the years since it was

postulated in the 1920s, although today, some psychologists still study it from the field of genetics and inherited behaviors.

Driving Theory

The driving theory has to do with the human being's balance and the concept of homeostasis.

This concept understands that human beings must have a certain balance. This balance allows it to function, understanding the human body as a circuit. We start in the morning and sleep at night. It requires energy to go through all your days.

Motivation has to do with it. The human being needs to satisfy needs. Taking certain behaviors and retracing a path leads you to fulfill a desire. Relieve that internal tension that is generated when there is a need.

When we are thirsty, we drink water. When we are hungry, we eat.

These types of motivations, these most primitive impulses, are of the order of the natural. We share them with the vast majority of the animal kingdom. The usefulness of this theory is that it covers all the most basic questions. It explains the engine that drives some behaviors and gives a theoretical framework to the strictly biological part. However, our species is peculiar because not all motivations stem from biological issues.

What happens when we keep eating, despite not being hungry? What mechanism acts in this case? The truth is that the complexity of the human body forces us to consider other options as well.

Arousal Theory

Our body needs to release doses of adrenaline from time to time. If you play sports, you will know. You know about the energetic potential activated when that adrenaline reaches the blood, the heart, and the brain.

This theory considers that people take different behaviors to manage and modify their arousal levels. It proposes humans evolved to carry a high level of arousal and that motivation is born from there.

According to this postulate, living like this is in our nature. Our evolutionary path, with its changes and adaptations, led us to this. However, there is no proper level of arousal. It is not something quantifiable.

Each of us will have our measure of what our bodies need and demand. And when you cover that demand, perhaps no more is needed. Some people, who live with high levels of arousal, sometimes need to reduce it. Contrarily, those with more laid-back personalities will look to increase their levels.

Humanistic Theory

To explain human motivations, it was necessary to give them a theoretical framework oriented toward the humanistic. Explain the cognitive reasons, which go beyond the field of the physiological. To do this, Abraham Maslow (1908-1970) created a system that ordered the needs of the human being and explained what mechanism motivates them.

How not to talk about Maslow? Did you think you could get rid of him? It is that his pyramid scheme to frame human needs concretely illustrates information that, for years, science has tried to quantify. He tries to give it a practical explanation.

Maslow's idea is that the needs of human beings are ordered by their complexity and evolve as they are fulfilled. This theory incorporates a hierarchical scale for necessities and the motivations that drive the desire to satisfy them.

In this way, there is a tendency for the human being toward mental health. To the extent that the most basic needs are met, new desires arise and, therefore, new impulses.

This complex process responds to the different levels of needs, which can be described, in the form of a pyramid, as follows: The basis of all human needs is physiological. Breathe, feed, and reproduce; primitive aspects of the human being. They are the first needs we had as a species and remain unchanged millions of years later.

Covering these issues is paramount to man's survival, and you'd be surprised how many people fail even to make it past this first step.

It is the foundation stone of the experience of being alive. To experience that process of daily homeostasis that we talked about earlier, where our body, with those basic requirements covered, has enough energy to function.

Security needs are the next rung of the pyramid, just above the most basic. Maslow describes them as protective measures.

He refers to the need to have a roof over our heads and shelter from the elements: the need to have financial security and sufficient resources to survive. Maslow also speaks of physical security, of caring for the state of man's health.

Once the human being has adequately passed these first two steps, the most basic and related to his physical integrity, the next step incorporates social needs. In it, the man has the opportunity to establish links and strengthen his family ties.

Integration is essential for a healthy life, and many daily motivations are strictly social. We adopt different behaviors, often according to habits and customs, to function in society. Both comply with the established rules and develop our emotional side.

These social needs (or affiliation) also involve a psychic structure built over millions of years by evolution.

Furthermore, it is also not intrinsically human. Scientists prove that an immense number of animals (primarily mammals or cetaceans) have complex social and family structures. Animals that, in the same order as man, first survive, then exist, and finally relate to each other. Who experience similar needs, and share these first three steps with us.

This also impeccably illustrates the mechanism of complexification of these needs to the extent that one steps up.

The next step in this pyramid is recognition of needs.

Here the structure begins to take on some desires strongly related to our species. Here we can say that the pyramid acquires its "humanistic" character.

These needs are related to the search for bonds of trust, the product of stable relationships, from which the human being tends to seek recognition, respect, and success.

Who do you think is more successful? A winning athlete or a good person? By what set of values do we measure success in life?

These needs constitute the psychological aspects of the human being. Satisfying them provides priceless value, translated into those sets of behaviors we take to live in society and bond with others.

Finally, at the top of the pyramid are the self-actualization needs. It is the area where, with the fundamental issues resolved, and the affective bonds established, we can give free rein to our desires.

There, man becomes spontaneous. Man becomes unique and unrepeatable. That's where we can free ourselves and start living what we want. Fulfill our desires, set our personal goals, and go for them. Perhaps they are professional goals, to grow in a job or study for a university degree.

They may also be personal, from everyday things like learning a language to infinitely more complex aspects. The truth is that this final step, which explains man's needs and the deepest root of their motivations, is key to the proper mental health of people. And the more we move within this zone, the better.

Expectancy Theory

This theory contemplates man's ability to plan for the future as an integral part of what generates their motivations. It suggests that thinking about what will happen and developing expectations about the future drives human beings to undertake. It motivates them to adopt behaviors that allow them to fulfill their objectives.

In this way, expectancy theory consists of three key elements.

Valence (the value that people assign to the potential outcome), instrumentality (if people believe that they have a role to assume and play to achieve the expected result), and expectation (the belief that one is capable of generating the expected result).

How to Develop a Winning Mindset

There is a significant first step in acquiring the mindset of a winner. Something that if you don't believe it, from the first moment, you can hardly move towards this goal. And it is to think that there are no limits. This premise to be incorporated must be adopted with devout faith, as a divine word, with the total dedication of the subject.

However, it is essential to understand what we mean when we say there are no limits to this mentality. It means incorporating persistence into your life. Stay focused with a clear goal, and be relentless in the face of adversity.

For winners, no excuses, setbacks, or adversities can stop

them. When they make a decision and have something in mind, they don't stop until they accomplish it.

It is understood that there will be many falls, many. When one plans a path, it is rarely fulfilled according to expectations. Some things go well, others fail. And it is natural. Winners understand mistakes as lessons to be learned as part of the very process of accomplishing the goal.

But the winner, who truly adopts this mentality, gets up and continues. In no way do they lose sight of their goal.

In addition to this initial, fundamental premise, those who incorporate a winning mentality into their lives must resolve conflicts quickly. Be aware of their faults and defects, and take responsibility for the problems.

This mentality is very dynamic and proactive. It is easy to create and innovate and build new paths, they love the unknown, and they like to take risks.

They prepare their steps in advance, thinks about them, analyzes them, and measures the possible results. They are people who prepare projects in the medium and long term, but in realistic terms. For this, it is ready, informed, and trained if necessary. They spend every minute of their time and every ounce of their brain on it.

There is indeed a random factor in the art of success. A small quota of luck that may or may not be had. It would be useless for you to be in the exact place and time for something good to happen if there are only limitations and a lack of security in your mind. However, prior preparation, concentration, and the right mindset will allow you to be more attentive. More awake to take advantage of even the slightest opportunity.

This is because they know what they want. It is clear in their mind. Crystal clear like water. A winning mentality helps build a strong character, as your way of reacting to pain is more rational. These people's goals are tangible, quantifiable, realistic, and within the expected scenarios. They know that, in large part, it depends on them to achieve it, which is essential for their behaviors, for the generation of motivation, which we talked about in the last chapter.

All this will be surrounded by empathy, cooperation, and a sense oriented to the common good without neglecting their interests.

Here are five concrete strategies to apply to your life to help you incorporate the winning mindset:

Being Talented Doesn't Make You Successful

As we saw earlier, the fixed mindset considers that you are destined for success just because you have talent. And we will see, throughout the book, that this is far from the truth.

The first mental exercise you must face to incorporate a winning mentality is understanding that it depends on your effort, work, and sacrifice. Understand that your talents will indeed serve you to reach the goal, but it would be a mistake to depend only on them. It does not work like this.

Those most confident in their talent are the first to be defeated. Because if you place all your trust in them blindly, in the first adversity that comes along, you will see that you have no resources left to fight it. You will have put all your eggs in one basket, that of your talent, which is unwise.

You cannot get out due to your talents from unforeseen events and challenging situations. Therefore, it is necessary that you trust your abilities but with your feet on the ground. You must give yourself body and soul to sacrifice and effort. That will be the path that leads to success.

That is the path chosen by the successful.

Start With Small Steps

Once you are convinced that, in addition to your talent, you have what it takes to be successful, it is time to take the initiative. Take those first steps toward your goal, whatever it may be.

To do this, I recommend that you start with small steps. Be realistic and practical. Starting with leaps and bounds is a risky move. It can give you great benefits, but also comes at a high cost. The winning mentality is acquired through other types of strategies.

Successful people take risks, to be sure, but they are calculated risks. Before making a move, they analyzed it a thousand times in their heads. They are intelligent, and they plan the possible results. Based on that planning and generated expectation, the mentality is strengthened. A safe space is created. It minimizes the risks and begins (little by little) to gain inertia.

This inertia, this first forward movement, may not be significant initially. As I say, it will be small steps that will bring you closer to the goal. There will even be some that don't necessarily get you closer, but help guide the flow at times of forks. However, as time goes by, the forward movement speeds up, builds energy, and becomes increasingly difficult to stop.

This impulse, this dynamic motivation, must be what makes you impervious to difficulties. And keep it on the rails of success.

Strengthen Your Character

Psychologists believe that strength of character is the most critical factor for success. Beyond talent and planning, if the person does not have the necessary character to sustain themself there, it will be difficult for them to achieve their goals.

This necessary integrity, this construction of an appropriate grit, will keep the subject on the road in moments of falls, doubts, and uncertainties. It must combine the person's persistence and commitment to the goal. Successful people form a strong bond between these two variables and share a passion.

Retracing your goals with these strengths dramatically increases your chances of achieving your goal and long-term success. It has to do with the ability to stay focused and focused, despite setbacks. Seize adversity as opportunities to learn and follow the path unperturbed.

It will be through the formation of character, tolerance to frustrations, and a constructive mentality regarding difficulties, that the successful man or woman is formed. That you advance with determination towards the goal. Insistent, resilient, inspired, and motivated.

Trust Your Vision, Trust Your Instincts

You may have a particular vision of things. A world's interpretation around your experiences, thoughts about how to proceed, and a specific goal to accomplish. These visions are always something personal. Incorporating a positive mindset into your life involves trusting your vision. Be sure that, with successes and errors, you decide which way to go towards your goal.

Of course, this does not mean becoming inflexible or uncompromising. On the contrary, the real challenge is to be honest with yourself, with what you want and feel is right, while listening to those who think differently.

Trusting your vision also means contrasting it with the other ideas. If you think that the best way to get to Newark is driving the Wittpenn Bridge, it's totally valid. But don't refuse the idea of going over the Hackensack River Bridge. You can stop for lunch in Little Tijuana and then continue your journey down Market Street.

What I am going with is that trusting your vision is essential, but being receptive to the vision of others will be of great help. It is up to you how much and how it will serve you.

Take Action

This is the most crucial part of the process, where most fail, and the filter becomes unavoidable. It is the moment of action. The moment when one must take everything learned and put it into practice.

Taking the initiative requires prior preparation. In addition to all the factors described, it also has to do with the courage to start the route. Every time we set a goal for our life, the path to it will be full of insecurities.

There will be hesitations, dilemmas to be resolved, and decisions to be made. Having enough courage to face those fears and sustain motivation over time will be necessary.

Many people meet the vast majority of the requirements, have things clear, trust their instinct, and prepare themselves by learning about the steps to follow. They have a clear objective and want to go for it. But they fail to get past this final stage. For various reasons, you cannot take that first step of putting everything you have seen into practice.

This is the first great filter between those who are successful and those who are not. And it is also the moment of truth. It is the moment that will have been waiting for you all this time. If you are prepared and feel safe and confident in your abilities, this moment will be easier for you.

INTERACTIVE EXERCISES

After analyzing Maslow's pyramid I decided to make a small balance on which step corresponded to me, applying it to my life, I discovered that I usually jump between steps. Some issues in my life feel resolved. For example, some wishes are fulfilled and achievements obtained. And others, I think that I lack a little.

There are often differences between how we feel about our lives and how we really are. This is because, sometimes, our perspective is not the right one, or we have some problem in our lives that shadows our analytical capacity. It dims our ability to appreciate the big picture. I invite you to carry out this reflective exercise.

It will help you to know where you stand. You will be able to consider which aspects of Maslow's pyramid you feel accomplished and in which you could be better. The more and better you know your own desires, the more likely you are to succeed. You must know well the context in which you expect them to be fulfilled, the road ahead, and the strengths of your own heart.

Put your life on Maslow's scale, and see the result.

As we have seen throughout this first chapter, the mentality one approaches their days is essential for success. And when we talk about success, we don't just mean sports. This writing invites you, the reader, to apply this type of mentality not only in your sports discipline, but also in everyday life.

A positive, flexible, and constructive mindset are a must-have to begin the path to change what we want and achieve the expected results. It must be a structural change, born from the most recondite place of your being. It must be a faithful expression of what you hope for your life.

By incorporating a positive, optimistic, overcoming mentality into your life, you will see good results will become evident. You'll see its evidence if your focus is improving your physical performance.

Next, we will talk about the power of the mind. How, unconsciously, the body follows it wherever it goes. We will discuss some strategies to train our brain and change it positively. Conceive the mind as a creative source of realities, and use it in our favor.

Now is the moment. Take Action.

A BONUS GUIDE:

3 THINGS ATHLETES SHOULD **STOP** DOING

2

WHERE THE MIND GOES, THE BODY FOLLOWS

There is a point in high-performance sports where the differences between competitors are drastically reduced. A level in which two great athletes have similarities. In their physical conditions, in what they train, how much they dedicate to their work, how much they perfect themselves, etc.

At this time, victory and defeat come down to mentality. A shot on goal that should have been a center, a curved ball that should have been straight. Those small differences in mentality, which influence you internally, can cost a fraction of a second in a race or lead you to make a wrong decision during a match.

Playing a sport involves a constant decision-making process. However long the activity lasts, the athlete must use their physical condition and their brain to reach victory. Because, in the end, everyone wants to win.

The physical conditions are, as well as attitude, energy

and concentration. I feel prepared to achieve it, and I'm going for it. However, all those factors can collapse in a second. Everything will be in vain if the mind does not accompany it.

Psychological armor before a race is essential. And in the case of Olympic athletes, many of them use the resource of visualization.

As in the case of the example, in the Olympic Games, all athletes are outstanding in their sport. All of them belong to the elite of their disciplines, and their high performance, individual and collective, leaves them relatively leveled.

The big differences are usually between nations. In the Olympic Games, the great powers of the medal table are usually those countries with an entire internal structure dedicated to assembling teams and training top-level athletes.

Visualization used by Olympians is all about gaining an edge over the competition. Beat the rival thanks to the power of images, expectations, and what this generates in us.

Kayla Harrison said that every night she visualized herself winning the competition. She stood at the top of the podium, watching in amazement her flag's hoisting, feeling the weight of gold on the back of her neck.

Visualization has immense motivational power. Not only is the expectation built, the potential outcome known, and it is imagined. It is seen, felt, and perceived. It must be a vivid, almost tangible experience.

Mentally prepare yourself for the possible outcomes. Another athlete, like the swimmer Missy Franklin, recognized that the pre-match visualization strategy helps reduce anxiety. "When I get there, I've already imagined what's going to happen a million times, so I don't really have to think about it," she told the New York Times.

Anticipate the play. Some visualize their own performance to improve their chances of success. Also, those who perform this exercise plan different strategies within the game. They try to be prepared to face different scenarios.

This exercise is literally incorporated into training. It is done mentally, in moments of inactivity, and is approached positively. Serious work is done on the aspects of the game, and the mental programming to achieve the objective. Below we will take a closer look at what visualization is, where its power lies, and what practical ways you can incorporate it into your life.

The Power of Visualization

Visualization is the act of visualizing. It refers to mentally developing the image of something abstract, giving visible characteristics to what is not seen, or representing issues of another nature through images. In this way, through this visualization, it is possible to achieve a representation of reality. In the same way, we cannot forget the existence of many other types of visualization.

Therefore, it is considered a way of finding well-being simply by resorting to what the mind is. It is established that thanks to visualization, there can be a reduction in stress levels, you can lose weight, your blood pressure can get lower, and you can decrease specific chronic pain.

The idea of creative visualization, on the other hand, is used in psychology. It is a motivational technique that invites a person to "see" in their mind what they intend to achieve.

Those who defend the validity of this technique affirm that creative visualization helps configure thought so that the subject guides their ideas and actions towards the goal. Suppose an athlete plans to run a marathon. In that case, therefore, they should engage in creative visualization and imagine what it would be like to cross the finish line.

The positive feelings generated by visualization can contribute to motivation.

All visualization requires a good imaginative flow to capture it. And the more vivid it is, the more effective it will affect the person.

For this, imagination as a creative process is essential. Allows the subject to manipulate their thoughts to create an image. It means forming this image without the stimuli of the environment, completing it only in your head, and making it capable of being perceived by the senses. Both the visual and the others.

As we mentioned before, being able to see the target, feel it in your hands, and hear it as if it were there.

Imagination allows us to form these mental experiences and take advantage of them. The visualization strategy has to do with taking advantage of its results and knowing its consequences. This visualization can be of childhood memories, imaginary or fantastic events, and future events.

Events that the subject imagines happening to prepare for the future motivate themselves or remove fears and insecurities.

It helps knowledge to be applicable in problem-solving and is essential to integrate the experience and the learning process. It is an abstract process that uses memory to relate information in non-factual ways. That is, the imagination takes previously perceived and experienced elements, transforming them into new stimuli and realities.

Imagination can be reproductive or creative. The first is when we visualize events from the past, from our history. Events that happened to us and that we can collect with memory. On the other hand, the creative images we create on our own.

Remember that what we think, we become. Suppose, in addition to thinking about it, we can see it on our mental screen, bring it to life and enjoy it as if it were already happening. In that case, we are creating what we visualize and bringing it to the present.

This step is vital for our life and material or spiritual prosperity. We can imagine material things and moods of happiness, peace, and harmony. We can also visualize the processes of our spiritual evolution and picture ourselves on the path to our objectives.

For this, we must follow five necessary steps for a complete visualization.

First, you have to determine what you want to manifest: Of course, let this be something honorable, constructive, and worthy of time and effort. Be sure what drives you to be better, and meet your goals. You must be honest with yourself and with the rest of the world.

Remember that there is a big difference between the use of desire and caprice. Take charge, discipline, and consciously control your inner being. Choose what you want to visualize in your mind, design, and make that plan manifest in your life.

You will then need to state your desired plan in words and out loud: as clear and concise as possible. Write it down ahead of time, so you don't forget any details. In this way, you will record your desire in the outside world, visible and tangible. The greater the intensity of the experience, the more detail is taken into consideration. The stronger the request, the better.

Once you are clear about your goal and have stated it strongly, it is time to close your eyes. Concentrate and try to see what you long for to be fulfilled within your mental screen. Contemplate being able to create, visualize, and create a picture within your own consciousness that represents your desires.

That ability is fundamental to incorporating a proper mindset into your life. Your conscience will drive you out to the outside world, the picture you see and feel within you.

A few years ago, my wife and I decided to emigrate to Barcelona, to live for a year and see how the city felt. A new life, with a new job, in a new town. A long process, very stressful, but that invited us to dream of unimaginable things.

I remember every night I put my little son to sleep in his

crib, closing my eyes and visualizing different moments ahead of him. It helped me significantly reduce the anxiety and fears typical of such a project.

Sometimes I visualized myself arriving at the airport and renting a new house. At other times, I imagined getting a new job or learning to speak the language. All things that I knew I had to do in the short term.

After making the visualization, read your plan or desire as often as possible during the day. Do it always before going to sleep because your mind can save that image and the sensations it produces in you.

This way, you can remember them later through your night dreams.

How It Enhances Sports Performance

It is understood that, to optimize your sports performance, the apparent approaches are training, conditioning, and practice. However, as we saw in the case of Olympic athletes, many use their mind power to fine-tune their abilities and gain a mental advantage over their competitors.

It is proven that these techniques help improve sports performance, backed by the power of the mind, by visualizing and building psychological strength. The world-famous athletes who used this technique are Arnold Schwarzenegger, Michael Jordan, and Michael Phelps. They have openly commented on their strategies. Psychologists and coaches agree that visualization's power can make a difference.

As we mentioned before, using visualization as a strategy to improve sports performance implies the use of all the senses. Not only see the ball enter the basket, but feel its texture in your hands and hear the characteristic sound going through the net. Give entity to visualization and surrender to its power.

Do it properly, thinking about the forms and the precise technique. Visualization should not only be graphic but controlled. The concentration level must be higher. And, of course, don't stop practicing.

These strategies we describe are only helpful if they are part of a whole. Athletes must practice and be disciplined and orderly in their training. Leave the physical in each practice, take care of yourself and be responsible for both you and your teammates.

Undoubtedly, mental toughness plays an important role in sports performance. In addition to visualization, mental toughness is another essential aspect of the mindset that cannot be ignored. Being able to push past physical distress thanks to your mindset is another way elite athletes can beat their competitors. Get a small (but decisive) advantage in ranked matches.

Like visualization studies, mental toughness can give athletes a competitive edge when combined with physical training.

To optimize your training and achieve significant improvements, consider working with experts trained in neurolinguistic programming or sports psychologists. They will be able to help you exploit all that potential and achieve more and better progress.

Building Mental Strength

Strengthening mental strength is essential to increase performance and will be a very personal variable. To begin with, each sport has specific moments where the game's strategy and the physical exhaustion appeal to the mind.

For example, the Argentine coach Carlos Bilardo (world champion in 1986 with Diego Maradona) said that soccer had 20 crucial minutes, where one could not afford to be distracted. Those minutes were the first 5 and the last 5 of each part. At that time, most teams scored their goals. In the first minutes, you risk entering the field of play unfocused, giving the rival that advantage. In the last minutes of the game, half of the brain of the athletes is usually already in the locker room, which has cost victories.

For example, a long-running race has its specific points where psychological integrity comes into play. I remember the last time I ran 10 miles. I had a breaking point where I thought I wouldn't make it. I was close to the finish line, maybe two or three more miles, but the racecourse forced me to pass over a long bridge.

As I regulated my breathing and the use of energy to get up that bridge, I convinced myself that going down it would be easier. Once down, though, I felt for the first time in the race that my legs wanted to leave me. While running in auto-

Where the Mind Goes, the Body Follows

matic mode, almost without thinking, I looked up and did not see the finish line in front of me—still a few miles to go.

At that time, I did not think about leaving, but I did think *and now what do I do?* I had to solve that problem; the only solution that occurred to me was a mental one—taking advantage of that acquired inertia to put one foot in front of the other and put my mind blank.

From that moment on, and for a while, I ran, looking at the asphalt. I didn't think about the landscape I was missing out or how far the goal was without thinking about raising my head and not visualizing it. I was mesmerized by the movement of my feet, by the rhythm of each step forward, and focused on nothing more than continuing that movement automatically.

But convinced that I would succeed. That was never in doubt.

After a few minutes like that, my mind snapped back into place. I raised my head, looked straight ahead, and managed to connect with the target. I regained confidence and concentration and completed the race without any problems.

But it was just a moment, unexpected adversity, that forced me to improvise. To find my way of coping with that situation. For the next race, I studied the route better. I could anticipate these issues. Honestly, I did not take the time to check the route at that time. I didn't find it necessary. It wasn't my first 10 miles, that's why I was overconfident.

What strengthens some could harm others. Each one

must know where that personal strength is and what steps to follow to bring it out in the necessary moments.

This strength is developed just like physical strength. It is practiced as part of complete training. I mean that it is multi-disciplinary. For this, you can practice overcoming daily discomforts, knowing yourself. Know what mechanism comes into action in our head when we have to solve problems. You will find that the very act of solving them will increase your confidence and self-esteem.

Only through strengthening your strengths and visualizing the success of your goals will you be able to discover the true inner power, the potential for action, and the wide margin for improvement in your performance.

Five Tips to Visualize Like an Olympian Athlete

As we have seen, top athletes in all fields of sport have their mind tricks to achieve successful results. Winning against their rivals from the mental aspects of the game.

This is not just physical practice. It doesn't just respond to the hundreds of hours a week that athletes dedicate to their training, but it is the result of mental exercise that you can practice yourself sitting at home or in the office while you work.

To do this, you must imagine your goals, those objectives you want to achieve, to create that image in your mind and thus attract it. Also, prepare your body and mental state so that you unconsciously tend to take the right path to success.

Visualizing should be a fun exercise. May it be easily

practiced and born from your deepest desires. Many people use this strategy for various purposes. Some have business goals for their businesses' success—others use this resource to change their habits or improve their physical condition.

If you're not already using visualization to drive success in your business, here are five simple steps to get started.

Know What You Want

This is a fundamental preliminary step, depending on the objective's clarity. How much do you know about it, and how much do you want? This factor must be clear to program the way to it successfully.

It will depend entirely on you. Know your thoughts, analyze and interpret your desires, and in this way, you will have a better chance of achieving them.

Keep It Specific

While many people have general visualizations for life goals and aspects of their trade or business, athletes' visualization is often more specific. What kind of technique to use for a three-point shot? How to locate the feet, and where to stand outside the painted area?

Create in your mind that image of the perfect shot. The flawless fall. Practice it there as many times as you can. Even memorizing the choreography of the movements, you need to comply with the desired technique perfectly.

Use Images

Beyond the mental and imaginative part of the visualization process, having tangible images of what you want can help bring intensity to the experience. Bring the rest of your senses into this exercise, and make visualization a transformative moment.

Don't Forget to Practice

Like any exercise, visualization needs practice. Make this exercise part of your routine. Take a specific moment of the day dedicated to this, and make the practice recur.

Stay open, be positive, and trust your own mind. If you practice this resource daily, you will see significant advances in the art of visualization (it will be more vivid and complex), and you will notice positive results quickly.

Combine Visualization With Training

Visualization will not replace practical work. Just like Olympic athletes, you still need to work hours to achieve results. But visualization can act like subconscious programming, bringing opportunities to your attention that you might otherwise miss.

Supplement the visualization with suitable workouts. Work with professionals trained in the subject, and invite your teammates to accompany you in this process. Make them part of your mental setup, and they will add tremendous value to the whole experience.

INTERACTIVE EXERCISES

To put this exercise into practice, find a quiet space in your home, and make yourself comfortable.

Close your eyes, and begin to breathe slowly and deeply. Focus your attention on your breath. Feel the sound of the air inflating your lungs, and your chest expands and contracts with each exhalation. Make the breath an ambient sound. Use it to relax, calm your anxiety, and focus on the goal.

Once you feel that absolute relaxation as if your body first weighs twice as much and then is light as a feather, imagine a place where you feel totally free. Where everything is just the way you want it. You're entering an idyllic world created by your mind to give you a holding space. It can be anywhere, in any context, as long as it helps you relax and makes you happy.

Focus the rest of your senses on the scene, and turn the experience into something tangible. Make it look natural. For example, if you imagine yourself sitting in a theater, surround the experience with as many details as possible. Think about the seat's velvet texture, the varnished wood finish of the armrests, and the carpet's texture under your feet when you walk.

Think about the lighting in the room and the noises that come from it. Think of a smell that transports you to this scene. Everything that increases the intensity of the experience will be welcome and allow you to put together a complete image.

Stay there, visualizing whatever is on your mind. Think of that beautiful feeling that the accomplished goal gives you. Think of your wishes, visualize them and see them come true. Connect your body and mind with these feelings that come from exercise.

Now open your eyes and connect that idyllic world with the real world. Take those sensations, feelings, and desires to the concrete plane. Take your goals for the day, and go for them.

At this point in the book, you are probably seriously considering the need to incorporate these mental strategies into our daily lives. To modify and optimize our performance, physical and mental, both in life and in sports.

Perhaps you want to lower your times and run faster and better. Or do it more efficiently, reducing energy consumption and optimizing your performance. Maybe you want to win a tournament or be in the top three. Make a podium, and overcome yourself.

If you practice the art of seeing yourself there, with the goal achieved, if you feel that satisfaction, and perceive that reality with most of your senses, the chances of achieving it increases considerably.

However, like any change process, it comes with its low points. Beyond all the energy, attitude, and impetus we face in our projects, there will be difficult moments. There will be failures, challenges, and frustrations.

In the next chapter, we'll first learn how to recognize anxiety when it strikes us. We'll differentiate it from the concept of fear; two similar ideas are usually strongly related. And we will also see different ways to use anxiety for good. It depends on us.

3

DEALING WITH SPORTS ANXIETY

In these modern times, anxiety has become a fairly common condition among most people. Whether due to issues related to stress, work, or economic problems, more and more people suffer from anxiety disorders.

And among them, high-performance athletes are not far behind.

Meet your goals, keep your sponsors happy, create a bond with your followers, and move skillfully on social networks. Today, being an elite athlete is not just about fulfilling your goals on the field.

There are athletes who show the world an unbeatable image. Still, many times (without showing it), they go through challenging situations that put them at the limit of their abilities and seriously affect their mental health. People don't notice it, but they live under very high pressure.

In 1996, soccer star Diego Maradona defined the immense differences between the pressures of athletes and those of the general public in one sentence: "There is pressure on someone who gets up at 5 in the morning and has to feed their family. We, footballers, drive around in BMWs and Mercedes-Benz."

With this quote, Maradona described a reality; the pressure of athletes has to do with performance on the pitch and with lighter issues off it. Rarely does an elite athlete compete for their life and their family. Rarely crossing the line a second later than your competitor will result in your kids not having a plate of food at the end of the day.

However, having made this difference, it is important to recognize that athletes' stress is there. It becomes evident when one of them loses their way with addictions, or their performance drops considerably, and they disappear from the international scene.

Among them, a clear example of overcoming is that of Kevin Love, who in 2018 shared his situation with the world and made visible a problem that most of the time remains under the rug. Admitting you have a problem is a sign of weakness in the competitive field.

He explained he had an incident during an early-season game against the Atlanta Hawks where he felt trapped and didn't know what was wrong. It wasn't until later that he identified this feeling as an anxiety attack.

However, Love's problem did not start there, but several years earlier, in 2012. That season he had broken his hand twice, and he had been almost entirely out of the competition. From that moment, he began to feel his whole life was falling apart and how he was sliding down a spiral that made him sick.

In his case, in addition to anxiety, Love had to deal with a strong picture of depression. He locked himself in his house and found no reason to leave. He turned away from his family and friends and began to retrace a challenging path. "The darkest period of my life," as he confessed to The Players Tribune.

Until then, Love believed he should not worry about mental health problems, that those things usually happen to others and not to you. He discovered (after that episode) that he had dealt with anxiety throughout his life, many times without knowing it or being aware of the problem. He wasn't ready to accept that weakness. He believed getting that reality would make him feel different from the rest. Weak compared to his rivals.

That night in 2018 was the breaking point. All of us suffer from anxiety fear, but it comes in one way or another. Anxiety is not a disease that can be treated by escaping from it. One must take an active stand against it. Face it squarely. Fight it day by day. Learn to manage it, administer it in small doses, and know your symptoms.

Love remembers lying on the locker room floor at halftime of that game, panting, and his heart pounding in his chest. He felt like he could die.

In these episodes, the visual field reduces, and one feels trapped. The heart begins to beat stronger to observe the muscle's movement through the chest. Every process of our body becomes torture. The air becomes so thin as if one were in the death zone of Everest. Breathing becomes difficult. One feels that the air enters and fills the lungs, but does not perceive the oxygen. The situation becomes desperate, and the subject becomes nervous. And inadvertently, all this cocktail only worsens the scenario.

Meanwhile, his coach asked him a fundamental question that everyone dealing with this problem must answer: What do you need?

It is crucial to know what we need to overcome this situation. Understand what our mind, our body, and our soul need. In some severe cases of anxiety and depression, the solution is chemical. You should consult with health professionals specialized in this type of condition, who will be able to give birth to different medications that help the subject.

Some overcome these obstacles through meditation. Others do some hobby that relaxes them and rediscovers their inner peace. In other, milder cases, the response is often internal. It is found in the deepest part of our being and takes various forms.

Beyond the fact that basketball helped Love distract himself, anxiety and depression took their toll on him. Little by little, he was undermining his psychological makeup until his body said enough.

From then on, his strategy to combat these feelings was to talk. He started therapy and found a safe place to express what was happening to him without fear of what they would say. He managed to show himself fully as a human being—no masks or costumes.

He understood that it was a healthy way to control those

negative emotions and served as a concrete strategy to overcome anxiety. Over the years, she learned to deal with the anxiety of her sports career in various ways. In this way, he became a spokesperson for mental health care in sports.

Sports Anxiety

We often come across athletes who feel very anxious. The symptoms they suffer from cause performance to decrease, which increases concern and, in turn, anxiety itself, generating a vicious circle in which the athlete sometimes gets stuck.

Anxiety in sports is often caused by the interaction between the personal factors of the athlete and the sport they practice. Each athlete's personality traits will make anxiety more or less recurrent. Some characteristics can generate pressure, such as the importance of a sports event, the uncertainty of competition, and personal factors, such as self-esteem or anxiety.

Sometimes they will be complex experiences, but they will transform the athlete's life (like the Kevin Love case described above), other times it will be episodes that can literally end an athlete's career.

What Is It?

By definition, anxiety is a negative emotional state that includes feelings of nervousness, worry, and apprehension, related to the activation or arousal of the organism. Thus, anxiety has a thought component, called cognitive anxiety, and a somatic anxiety component, which constitutes the degree of perceived physical activation.

As the activation of the nervous system increases, the body secretes adrenaline into the bloodstream, increasing heart rate, breathing, and muscle tension. This reaction is our body preparing itself to increase its response capacity during stress and nervousness.

However, extreme nervousness can cause the body to continue secreting adrenaline, much more than the necessary dose, which generates a state of blockage in its ability to respond to the situation. At this time, an athlete will see how his performance drops, creating more worries and increasing his state of stress and degree of activation.

Causes

For example, it is especially common in athletics to see cases of anxiety and stress. It responds to several reasons: it is a sport practiced in different ways and different situations. Sometimes it is practiced individually, and other tests are collective or by teams. Some competitions allow the athlete to move at a leisurely pace, while others require sprinters.

Sometimes high levels of anxiety occur due to the expectations that other teammates or the coach have of the athlete, generating stress for the competition. Some tests require tactics and preparation, and when the time comes for the race, feeling insecure and nervous can mean that the performance is not as expected.

Arousal refers to the organism's general physiological and psychological activation, which occurs in the form of variable intensities along a continuum that is observed from deep sleep to frenzy, panic, or intense anger. When we talk about sports practice, arousal will be defined as an energizing function responsible for taking advantage of the body's resources in the face of vigorous and intense activities.

What Increases the Risk of Suffering It?

According to a World Health Organization study done in March 2022, it is estimated that more than 25% of the world population suffers from some symptoms related to anxiety without knowing it. This number skyrocketed after the pandemic and lockdown. Sport is no exception. In cases where a sport is practiced, the difference between success and failure can be minimal, predisposing the athlete to a high-stress level.

To begin with, the risk of suffering anxiety related to sports activity will have to do with a state of excessive tension, which manifests itself permanently in the athlete's life. It extends beyond their own strength, fully impacting the athlete's physical, behavioral, and psychological plane.

This implies a situation of chronic exhaustion, of a subject who lives his life in constant effort. These athletes do not rest because when they are not training, they are using their energy to think about what they will do to improve their performance.

The emotional tension, overwhelm, and fatigue of these people have a physical limit. Once they pass that point, the body begins to take its toll. In addition to physical and mental conditions, this state of constant emotion alters the athlete's life and everyone around him.

There is a point in this whole chain of adverse events when the athlete gets used to the mental rhythm that stress and anxiety provoke. They incorporate it as part of their life and slowly attacks his state of mind. Finally, the subject collapses, and all the adaptation strategies served him up to that moment will cease.

Each athlete is from a different world. Some of them may perceive the same situation in different ways. Perhaps they do not get the time necessary to qualify for a test and feel like a resounding failure despite giving their all. While another athlete, faced with the same situation, could consider it part of the learning process. And give it an optimistic framework.

However, the difference between everyday anxiety and sports is that sports' anxiety has a considerable history of physical and neuropsychic load in training sessions and competition, constantly under pressure. In this sense also, each athlete has a different degree of activation than the others.

Personal factors must be taken into account, since there are people who require a higher degree of activation for a task and others who can perform the same way with less activation.

Anxiety vs Excitement: What's the Difference?

Excitement and anxiety are two emotional states that are often characterized by intense and powerful feelings. However, there is a fine line between feeling excitement and feeling anxiety. When we find ourselves in these states, it is common to experience a feeling of being overwhelmed. Those things that excite us usually cause us a little anxiety too. And it is important to differentiate both feelings.

Emotion is a natural state when some experience, project, or event that motivates us comes along the way. In turn, it can be defined as a powerful, intense feeling that generates sensations inside us that are impossible to ignore.

What was the last thing that generated emotion in your life? Maybe you were able to change jobs and get that position you wanted so badly. It could also be some family event, such as the birth of a son, nephew, or grandson. That intense feeling inside us that we need to shout from the rooftops what our heart dictates means that it is exciting.

In the same way, emotion can be caused by sad or traumatic events in our lives. The same intensity that we talked about, but enhancing unpleasant feelings. Perhaps you failed a big test, got into a fight with a friend, or suffered a recent family loss. When the emotion is negative, the mechanism activated in the body is the same. The consequences are simply different. Our body does not process positive and negative in the same way.

Retracing this path, we can define what it means to feel excited. However, identifying this fine line between emotion and anxiety can be challenging. Since processing excitement (whether or not positively), all the mood factors that come into play link to feelings of anxiety.

For example, when we cross that line and turn emotion into anxiety, that positive feeling can turn into impatience, also, in cases where emotion leads us to anticipate events. Waiting for something so eagerly that, if the final result is not what we expected, we feel disappointed and lose enthusiasm with the fear that our expectations will not be met. This removes the joy from our emotions and turns them into something negative. It makes us anxious.

When we reach that point where happiness does not correspond to emotion, we have passed the point of no return. One can try to control that situation and reduce the damage, but the feelings of disappointment have already hit you.

Emotion is a feeling from which you can hardly return. Once these sensations hit the door, there will be no effective containment strategy against them. Excitement is beautiful when we can enjoy the energy and have fun with the sentiment.

Sometimes the emotion and expectation are so great that the enthusiasm is maintained until the moment the objective is fulfilled or the events unfold. And then our emotional state changes. It was not what we expected. This change disconnects us from the experience that generated so much emotion in us. We lose the possibility of enjoying it. As if, previously, we had burned the ships.

Many times, the emotion arises from the expectation created around a specific result. The success of a project, fulfilling a wish. And if things don't turn out the way we expected (they rarely do), that essential change we hoped for in our lives doesn't come true. Or at least not immediately.

In those cases, our first impulse is probably to put emotion aside. Let it fade, thanks to the loss of enthusiasm. It's natural, but I invite you to consider another alternative. One that allows you to preserve that emotion and transform it as events unfold. Regardless of their final result.

To begin with, avoid giving the emotion more entity than it should. It's perfect to feel enthusiastic and generate expectations, but everything is in its healthy measure. If we feel that the pendulum of emotions takes us to the field of anxiety, we must transform that feeling there. Could you return it to its original state? Return into excitement.

Relabeling Anxiety as Excitement

The feelings of excitement and anxiety are almost identical. Both raise the heart rate and generate that feeling in the stomach, only comparable to those butterflies that we felt when we were children. Both can be linked to the physiological preparation your body experiences when it knows something new, different, or unknown is coming.

It's similar to when we bump into each other on the

street. As we fall, entirely unconsciously, the body prepares for the impact. As if it knew before we did.

Our behaviors, acts, and decisions start from a base of joy and emotion and are not driven by fear. However, beyond the similarities, there are feelings that evoke different sensations. Excitement is related to pleasure, while anxiety is directly related to fear. Awareness of this difference is crucial to giving our lives the proper framework.

This difference will allow us to enjoy every day as it should. In addition, psychologically, we will be better predisposed to recognize new opportunities and take advantage of them without the ballast of fear behind them.

Fear is not bad. It is a valid feeling, often allowing us to proceed cautiously. Be careful. Fear forces us to think about things twice (or more) times. Usually, though these sensations, one acquires security whether to decide or undertake a project.

It is a feeling that adds value as long as it does not control every aspect of our lives. Don't become chronic and flood every decision-making. It's okay for him to be a co-pilot for some situations, but never let him drive our destiny.

In this way, since both emotion and anxiety have marked similarities, it is necessary to learn to identify their symptoms. Learn to read our thoughts and interpret what mechanism is activated in us when one of them comes into action.

In case it is an emotion, keep it alive and take advantage of it. Turn it into something positive. But if we recognize patterns of anxiety, it will be necessary to change those feelings. Take them back to the field of emotion.

To do this, we must know ourselves internally and develop a high sense of emotional intelligence. That will be the critical tool, the ace of spades, to move forward.

Instead of fighting anxiety head-on, a better approach is turning that feeling into emotion. People who try this strategy are more likely to be successful. Persistent anxiety has been linked to physical illnesses and disorders, including gastrointestinal conditions and heart disease. Anxiety becomes problematic when it is chronic.

This mainly means having a pessimistic attitude at all times, living with the glass half empty. This mindset prevents seeing opportunities for positive change. Therefore, it contains growing, evolving, and projecting emotions healthily with joy and expectation well channeled.

Relabeling those anxious feelings and turning them back into emotions takes effort on our part. We will see below different strategies to achieve it.

There may be situations that only generate anxiety. In those cases, there will be nothing to do except deal with it in the best possible way. However, on other occasions, one has the freedom to choose the approach we want to give to our feelings.

These situations are opportunities to demonstrate our ability, how much we know ourselves, and how much good we can do ourselves. In these cases, the emotion must be an impulse that allows us to concentrate on the possible results and that pleasant feeling after calming our anxieties.

In this way, the best option is to concentrate on the positive results. Conceive the process that optimistically excites us to avoid wasting our energy thinking about everything that could fail. This is where anxiety takes hold. Being more excited will help you better choose the next steps. This will make success more likely.

In addition, it helps to understand from the outset the inescapable reality that some things will fail. Be aware of this, and anticipate that things never go 100% as planned. This way, when something fails, you will already know this situation. You will have foreseen its impact and can adequately anticipate it, minimizing its negative consequences.

Personally, when I feel anxious for any reason, I usually use that energy to go for a run. It works for me to channel it there. Drop all that anxiety with every step, and I feel better as soon as I finish the race. Maybe I didn't solve the cause of that anxiety, but it sure doesn't affect me the way it used to. The mind relaxes.

Take some time to relax. Part of being anxious is caused by being on the go all the time. Make sure you take time to rest, both your body and your mind. Dedicate a small moment of your day to do some activity that brings you peace.

Living with anxiety healthily and finding ways to use those feelings positively involve, as we mentioned earlier, developing a strong sense of emotional intelligence in your life. For this, it is essential to know each other. So we can deal with anxiety.

Coping With Sports Performance Anxiety

In the world of sports, performance anxiety is the one that attacks athletes in the moments leading up to a major competition. There, the nerves are felt with an unusual intensity. And it is not bad to feel nervous or anxious. It is the way our body has to tell us that we are ready. But excessive nervousness can affect our performance and, therefore, the expected results.

Some people become paralyzed with nerves. Others momentarily lose the ability to perform their sport correctly. There is a direct relationship between anguish by stress due to performance and our body's rejection. Sometimes, it negatively influences the decision-making process or performance in general. For this reason, Johns Hopkins Institute teaches athletes that anxiety is a normal, helpful feeling and that they must be predisposed to live with it.

We must first identify when these feelings occur to anticipate the possible consequences of sports anxiety. The symptoms are characteristic: muscular tension, rapid movements, errors in the technical execution of the discipline that is practiced, or aggressive demonstrations. Perhaps the clearest example of this type of reaction can be seen in tennis, when the player smashes their racket against the ground. This shows their state of mind, their impotence for some play. The only way to discharge this tension is to destroy his racket. What is at hand.

Dealing with sports anxiety is also about your ability to plan. However, keeping to the original idea and sticking to the game plan helps reduce stress. Maintain the degree of concentration necessary to act under pressure, and recalculate (if required) your action plan, that strategy you thought of before the match. This way, you will know what to do beyond any unforeseen event.

Stay positive. Try to surround yourself with people who reinforce those feelings, that optimism, and you will see positive results. You'll feel your self-esteem increase and thoughts that contribute to anxiety decrease. Be your first critic, but do so constructively.

And remember to breathe. Breathing is an essential part of self-regulation. Take deep inhalations and slow exhalations. And focus on relaxing. Anxiety will automatically reduce, allowing you to overcome that fear of sports failure.

INTERACTIVE EXERCISES

In sports, there will always be some stress; therefore, it is important to know how to handle it. Next, we will see several techniques to practice when you play sports. It will be essential to know which of them will make you better.

Deep breathing: using the resource of breathing is one of the first steps to containing stress and trying to relax. Deep breathing connects us with aspects of our interior. It is a practice that is designed to make you aware of your breathing, and the act of breathing becomes therapeutic.

Take a deep breath, and feel your lungs fill with air. Feel the sound of the air through your body, your chest getting bigger, and your abdominal muscles stretching.

And once you have breathed in, hold your breath for 5 seconds. Then exhale slowly. Take your time. Do it with your mouth half closed, slow. Repeat this exercise five times. It will help you relax, lower your heart rate and align your ideas.

Muscle relaxation: Find a comfortable, quiet place in your home and lie on the bed or sofa. Be aware of how your body weight sinks the mattress. Also, feel how the chest moves each time you breathe.

Begin to contract a group of muscles forcefully. Keep them contracted for about five seconds, and then relax them. Repeat the exercise five times, then move on to a different group of muscles.

To finish, relax your body and mind and go through each sector, relaxing your muscles. Until that weight that at first sank, the mattress becomes lighter and lighter.

Go to your happy place: This visualization often effectively reduces anxiety and stress. You should imagine a calm and peaceful place or situation. Feel the stress leave your body.

Security anxiety. Take a deep breath and exhale; when you do, you'll trade stress for relaxation. Repeat this process until you feel calm.

Mindfulness: Through this technique, the idea is to achieve a level of absolute concentration, physical and mental. Concentrate energy, and channel thoughts. Control stress or anxieties and focus on the present without worrying about the past or future.

Mindfulness allows you, among other things, to become

aware of everything that is under your control. This way, you will begin to feel that you have stopped worrying.

Those things, where the result depends on you, those under your radar, you have it under control. As for what is totally out of your control, you have no reason to worry. Because, in effect, you'll not influence the final result.

Create a routine: Having a routine for your life is essential to control (or even reduce) stress. As we saw earlier, this feeling is directly associated with fear. And among them, the fear of the unknown is usually paralyzing for most people.

The routine allows you to gain some degree of control over the variables. It gives you a frame of reference for spending most of your days. Focus on it. There will be no big shocks. There should not be. You will be able to focus on the routine and reduce the factors that generate stress.

Stay positive: Be optimistic about the future and your possibilities. Trust in your ability to cope with whatever situation has you down. Stay active and receptive, and surround yourself with people with the same attitude.

You will see that the more you get feedback from positive people, the better you will feel. And that feeling, as part of your daily routine, will allow you to take advantage of new and better opportunities.

Sport makes sense only if the athlete enjoys himself. If you learn the lessons, every discipline has to give. Yes, from healthy competition, you can build strong links. Friendly. Sincerely, whether practiced professionally or amateurishly, it should be a space for enjoyment.

Sports must be where the athlete leaves all their energy,

desires, and deepest fears. Where they can connect with the most primitive aspects of themself, but at the same time, the dynamics of competition force them to think. It forces them to use their mental resources to achieve victory.

If you are happy doing sports, if you are enriched by the experience and feel what I am telling you... then you will be able to manage your stress levels properly. That is an expected, natural, and controllable feeling.

So far, we have seen the logical way to modify our mind, body, and life structurally in different ways that lead to the same goal.

As we saw in this chapter, anxiety is a double-edged sword. It can be our worst enemy, literally ruining all our attempts to improve as athletes. It can be decisive when closing a race, defining a penalty, or hitting a home run. It may be the only difference between the winner and the loser, and between meeting our goals or not.

The idea is to transform that anxiety into excitement. Convert it into energy that feeds the engine of life. It's not easy, that's clear. It is not a walk in the park to achieve substantial changes in this aspect. Mishandled anxiety is corrosive. Mismanaged stress is poisonous.

Therefore, we will see positive results if we follow the right course and organize our minds through the different strategies seen in the chapter to reduce and control anxiety levels.

But for this, we must become mentally strengthened humans in addition to the exercises. We must know our potential, believe in ourselves, and know that there will be failures.

Success depends on how we deal with those failures and under what conditions we get off the ground. There is the key to all this. The attitude, mentality, and integrity with which we process the blows and the construction of a resilient character.

4

SELF-BELIEF AND RESILIENCE

Most athletes who achieve high success and fame tend to be very clear about self-confidence. It is usually a part of them, an aspect that accompanies them at all times. They are established athletes who built their careers based on sacrifice to stand out in the competition and be better than their rivals.

Of course, getting it is not easy. Nobody gives these athletes anything for free. They must strive at every moment to outperform their competitors. To do this, these people have high physical, technical, and mental development. And in case you overcome them, stay above them.

Be completely convinced of your capabilities. There is no impostor syndrome here. These athletes conceive of self-confidence as the security of feeling that one is up to the task at hand. They feel deep in their hearts (they know it as a universal certainty) that they can live up to expectations.

Physiological states can reduce feelings of confidence

through phenomena such as muscle tension, palpitations, and butterflies in the stomach. The bodily sensations associated with competition must be perceived as facilitating performance, which can be achieved by applying appropriate stress management interventions.

You probably know someone whose self-confidence has this unshakable quality, whose ego withstands even the biggest setbacks. In such people, trust is such a resilient quality. However, you can become arrogant if you live without being careful about your confidence levels. And in sports life and high-level competition, arrogance comes with its costs.

To build adequate self-confidence, the athlete must know that failure is always a possibility in the equation. Those who remain at the highest level in each of their disciplines do not achieve it by being perfect. Nobody is.

Although sometimes it may not seem like it, they are human beings. With all that that implies. They are people who have good days and bad days—better performances and games where nothing goes right for them. In addition to that, they may have health issues that affect them before a competition (it was the case with Ronaldo Luiz Nazario—the real "Ronaldo"—on the night before the 1998 France World Cup Final).

The most significant source of self-confidence is part of your emotional state. It has to do with controlling the emotions of competition, such as anxiety, expectations, and pressure. The more important the instance you compete, the greater the intensity of these sensations.

There will be moments of doubt and thoughts of insecurity that do not collaborate with forming the athlete's confidence. It will be important for him to be able to control these thoughts. To dose them.

Many factors can put an athlete out of competition. It affects their self-esteem, performance, and relationship with the public.

David Beckham, for example, went through it in 2004.

Beckham wasted a decisive penalty kick in that year's European Cup. He was a world-class midfielder, an eminent free-kick taker (and Victoria's husband). After the World Cup and the Champions League, this European cup is the most important soccer competition. It occupies third place in the ranking, and all the players want to win it with their respective teams.

In that match, England and Portugal drew 1-1 in regular time, scored one more goal each in extra time, and ended with a 2-2 result. Extending the definition to kicks from the penalty spot.

There, Beckham did not even kick the decisive penalty, but instead set out to execute the first of his team's penalties. However, as team captain, fans expected him to perform well at that key moment.

David missed, and his team started the penalty shootout at a disadvantage. However, one of Portugal's kickers also missed his penalty, and the series was tied. However, Beckham's shot was so bad that his performance hit the entire team's confidence from the first moment.

On the contrary, the confidence of the Portuguese goalkeeper (Ricardo) was better than ever. He held the decisive penalty kick (kicked by Vassel), gave his team the victory, and eliminated England from the competition.

Beckham's failure wasn't decisive, but it destroyed his entire team's mood and concentration. Their rivals already had half the victory in their pockets from then on—the mental one. As for the event itself, that penalty was so treacherous that the ball from that shot was saved by a fan and auctioned years later, reaching the figure of 10 million euros on eBay.

The Complex Art of Believing in Yourself

The path that leads to building adequate self-confidence is not easy. It requires effort and sacrifice and implies that one fully lends oneself to the experience. We must analyze our mind, our heart, and our body.

If you have a good level of self-confidence, you must explain what it is responding to. What mechanisms of our life and our way of being build and strengthen that confidence in ourselves? Performance achievements are known to be the biggest contributor to confidence in sport. When you perform any skill successfully, you'll build confidence and be willing to try something a little more difficult.

These people understand you should organize that skill learning into a series of gradually progressing tasks that allow you to master each step before moving on to the next. As we mentioned in previous chapters, running is impossible if we first don't learn how to walk.

Those of us who find ourselves on the other side of the street, on the opposite side of the road to self-confidence, must work twice as hard to acquire adequate levels of self-esteem. It does not come naturally to us, but implies a conscious and constant effort. We must pay particular attention to our triggers. To that which diminishes our confidence, our security, and our self-esteem.

Self-confidence has been proven to improve the performance of the vast majority of athletes. Many studies on the subject have shown that the level of confidence and the level of sports performance are directly proportional. Even under strictly controlled conditions, it has been demonstrated that performance is significantly affected when trust is manipulated (for better or worse).

The art of believing in oneself is complex. It has to do with how we perceive our own life and existence. Also, with the expectations, we create for ourselves. Where do we want to go? How do we want to do it? Do we have dreams or desires to fulfill? What stops us?

Believing in oneself also means knowing ourselves. We must know our physical and mental limits and our body and its signals. Be aware of both our limitations and those high points that make us stand out from others.

And also know our fears. Take charge of them, responsible for what they generate within us and how much they affect our performance in life and sports.

The Athlete's Worst Fears

In addition to all the internal work, all the effort, and self-knowledge involved in maintaining sports performance despite nerves and anxieties, it was shown that family and social support also positively affect the athlete's mind.

It reduces the effects of competitive stress and anxiety levels and increases the athlete's confidence. To do this, more and more coaches take the mental preparation of their coaches as a determining factor. Even preparing them from an early age. This way, they can build their career based on a good state of mental health and become adults ready to deal with the demands of the environment.

Since a child begins to practice a sport, they already start to develop their own resources and strategies. For this reason, working on young athletes' mental and psychological aspects is so important.

However, the athletes' fears are a reality that every coach must know how to deal with.

When we think of the fears of high-performance athletes, we refer to those concerns that attack them in the moments before a competition.

Tokyo 2020 made it possible to better understand that high-performance sport exposes athletes to situations of enormous stress and pressure. Every athlete is different and deals with competitive stress differently.

There are people with a tendency to suffer from mild problems. In contrast, other people can fall into depression and anxiety disorders. Therefore, it is essential that the athlete knows himself and adapts strategies to counteract the psychological effects of anxiety.

"I am not comfortable speaking in public, and I feel an immense anxiety when I have to address the world press," said Japanese tennis figure Naomi Osaka. She was fined for refusing to give press conferences at Roland Garros.

Pre-competitive anxiety and the uncertainty of the result are usually the most common fears. The fear of not performing like in training, not meeting expectations, not living up to what others expect.

The truth is that an elite athlete's psyche is the same as any person's. The difference is in the way of thinking and feeling. Elite athletes optimize neural connections to the maximum, automating their sport's most critical technical movements. They must be experts in making the most of their own resources, physical and mental.

When the athlete understands that the real competition starts against themself, their daily improvement will be their success. That's when they begin to work on their continuous improvement system to achieve the best version of themself, whatever it may be.

In sports, too much importance is given to winning or losing. It can go from success to failure in seconds, and the athlete must learn to properly manage his expectations and adapt to the different situations he will have to live in.

Each sport has its peculiarities and mental demands. Some require more precision, others more concentration, etc. However, individual sports require more ability and mental strength. In team sports, responsibility is more diluted, but other variables, such as leadership, cohesion, or group coordination, come into play. The important thing is to adapt the resources to the different needs of the athlete and take care of the environment.

Let's Define Resilience

It is the ability to adapt to adverse situations, positively transforming their consequences. Initially, it was interpreted as an innate condition, which was later taken into consideration not only individual factors but also the subject's family, cultural, and environmental factors.

Resilience is currently understood as the ability to succeed in a way acceptable to society despite stress or adversity, normally involving a serious risk of negative outcomes. It is also defined as a process of competitiveness where the person must adapt positively to adverse situations.

During the last two decades, the field of psychology has become interested in resilience, after several studies showed how some children who experienced extreme and traumatic situations during their childhood did not develop any mental problems or criminal behavior later.

According to the psychologist Catherine Moore, these children managed to become healthy and functional adults, despite the terrible adversities they had to go through, and they caught the attention of psychologists. For this reason, it is interpreted that there are different levels of resilience. Some people will be more likely to overcome these life challenges without problems. In contrast, others will see their behaviors and decisions affected by these traumas.

Resilient people know how to maximize results with what they have at hand. They can see opportunities where others see problems and have a mindset that allows them to use these opportunities for their own benefit.

They are usually optimistic, but not so much. They overcome difficulties without generating too much expectation in the results. They also have an overall development of their common sense. This way, they can interpret and channel the events of their lives for good.

How Resilience Impact Sports?

Resilience is a fundamental quality in any sport. Injuries are, among many factors, the greatest adversity an athlete will face. Athletes have to deal with the stress of competitions and the pressure of being the best at their job. To this, we must also add the concern for working with one's own body and the truth often hidden behind medals: elite sport often punishes the body.

For those who do not practice it professionally, sport can become a tool to train some psychological aspects. Resilience, among them.

For athletes, however, most pressures are self-imposed. It is also worth recognizing that many have no choice but to self-manage them. However, the obligation to deal with these pressures provides them with maturity that allows them to develop and strengthen their resilience. Thus, they become committed people with great determination. They also develop the faith that comes from having lived through many storms and knowing the clouds withdraw.

Let's think that athletes suffer from injuries, performance problems, and illnesses that can leave them unable to carry out their work. However, despite this, many of them bounce back from setbacks. For some athletes, overcoming an injury can be the biggest challenge of their careers. It is not easy. It often involves a huge physical and mental effort.

However, their mental strength will allow them to stay afloat when others sink. It is the product of their experience, but also an exercise in commitment and perseverance.

INTERACTIVE EXERCISES

There are different strategies to optimize self-confidence levels and apply them in sports. Here are three specific exercises you can practice in your daily life. You will notice positive results in a short time, controlling your anxieties, reducing your insecurities, and strengthening your self-esteem.

Exercise 1: Recognize the advantages and disadvantages.

To achieve stability in your confidence, knowing exactly what mobilizes it is necessary. Take a sheet of paper and divide the page into two columns. Label the first column "high trust situations" and the second column "low trust situations."

In the first column, list all the situations or circumstances in your sport where you feel completely safe. Those moments that you know you can respond appropriately will be positive to provide you with more security.

Instead, in the second column, list the situations or circumstances that sometimes cause your confidence to drop.

Identifying situations that make you uncomfortable is the first step in building greater self-confidence. This should have served to increase your awareness of areas for improvement.

Exercise 2: Visualize the focus of success.

This visualization exercise recreates the state of mind associated with successful sports performance. It will help you bridge the gap between your ability and confidence.

Imagine a huge spotlight shining on the ground. Now think back to a time in your sports career when you performed to the best of your ability. Think and reconstruct every move you make. Analyze what produced a successful outcome.

Looking at you from the outside, examine each of your five senses. See yourself inside the circle and standing out. Imagine exactly what the "you" inside the process is seeing, hearing, feeling, and smelling.

Now step into the spotlight and become a full partner to experience the events through your own eyes and in real-time. Once again, notice what you are seeing, hearing, and feeling. Notice exactly how this feels, so you can replay it at will whenever your confidence is slipping.

Exercise 3: Exploit your opponent's weaknesses.

Self-Belief and Resilience

Your opponent will have doubts and fears. Like any human being, they are susceptible to anxiety, tiredness, and indecision. If you spend time thinking about your opponents, focus on what weaknesses and fragilities you could most easily exploit.

Study images of your opponents and recognize the factors that negatively influence their performances. They may not be able to perform under certain conditions or have specific issues to consider.

In team sports, identify easily upset players and determine what makes them angry. What distracts them and takes them out of the competition.

A clear example of this strategy was experienced in the 2006 World Cup. The Italian defender Marco Materazzi, albeit quite controversially, used this technique in the tournament's final against his opponent, the Frenchman Zinedine Zidane. He allegedly insulted his sister, which caused a violent reaction from the French athlete, and he was expelled. France lost its captain and suffered a severe emotional blow. The final result? Italy champion.

We already have the structure. We have the tools. We have already traveled a path of teachings, learning, and changes. It is time to harvest our crops.

Reaching the point where we are is an important milestone. It means that you have managed to change your mentality and transfer that change of perspective to your body. In this way, dispose of, unconsciously, to success.

We are being honest with ourselves, knowing our strengths and weaknesses, and knowing irrefutably where we are right and where we are not. From there, we begin to achieve our goals and generate realistic expectations.

Bad channeling of anxiety is also a thing of the past. We have already learned to recognize it and use it in our favor. And according to what was discussed in this chapter, believing in ourselves and assimilating life's blows as part of the learning process is key—Mark the difference.

Next, we will dive into emotional intelligence—the idea of the maturation of our mind and heart.

The truth is that, as the years go by, we change. We learn, mature, and incorporate new things that make us (for practical purposes) different people.

A good level of emotional intelligence must accompany this maturation. Become the protagonists of our history. In this way, you can sustain the effort and improve yourself sportingly.

5
BECOMING EMOTIONALLY INTELLIGENT

Emotional Intelligence: an Overview

The concept of emotional intelligence (EI) arises as an attempt by psychology to explain intelligence factors that do not depend on the intellect. It tries to explain those samples of reasoning capacity, common sense, and panoramic vision of some people to get along in life and that there are not questions incorporated academically.

People with immense potential for action and who have acquired adequate emotional strength. It is not knowledge gained in a classroom exploring the details of the theory. Rather, they are practical day-to-day applications.

We must think of emotional intelligence as a construction of our mind that helps us understand how we can intelligently process and interpret both our emotions and the emotional states of others. This aspect of the human psychological dimension plays a fundamental role in our way of socializing and in the strategies of adapting to the environment we follow.

It has to do with a person's ability to observe their environment regarding emotions. It implies receptivity, understanding, generosity, and above all, empathy. Understanding the other is as essential as understanding oneself. That characteristic of how we relate to others, expressing and controlling our emotions, and understanding the emotions of others, will be key to success.

In purely sporting aspects, EI will be a fundamental tool to support the body and spirit in difficult times. Some experts even suggest that it may be more important than IQ in your overall success in life.

The IE cultivation is a hard and endless road because one can never be "totally intelligent." Intelligence is like a muscle that must be trained every day, at all times, until the end of our lives.

The information we collect through EI is key to responding to daily demands. Both personal and social ones. It makes men versatile, adaptable, and able to live in society. Specific goals, breaks, and impulses build the experience we call life.

Emotional Intelligence in Sports

Emotions play a vital role in our daily lives. Let's think carefully about the importance of emotions in them. We will quickly realize that there are many occasions when they have a decisive influence on our lives, even if we do not realize it. And in sports, incorporating EI as a tool requires conscious and oriented practice.

It requires an awareness of one's own emotions. It is necessary to drive our emotional reactions and complete or replace the behavior program with a response oriented to the game and the needs of the moment of the sporting event. To do this, every great athlete pursues goals such as persevering and enjoying learning. Build self-confidence and be able to cope with defeats. This is the only way to increase his chances of success.

Sport is a way to learn emotional intelligence, and athletes who manage these competitions will improve their sports performance. The intrinsic relationship between these variables makes most high-performance athletes take their emotional state and mental health seriously.

It is worth saying that each person will have a different domain of their emotions. This quality is usually very personal. There are people with this facet who are significantly more developed.

In addition, there is an inversely proportional relationship between traditional and emotional intelligence. Some people with high logical and analytical performance have been shown to lack the social characteristics that signify a good degree of emotional intelligence.

On the other hand, we can find people whose intellectual capacities are very limited. However, they manage to lead a successful life—both in the sentimental and professional fields.

Enhance Your Emotions, Enhance Your Performance

To incorporate emotional intelligence into your daily training routine, you must meet some basic requirements. Analyze your own heart in search of the elements of emotional intelligence. In this way, the psychologist Daniel Goleman (a pioneer in the study of EI) recognizes five fundamental aspects to consider:

- self-knowledge or emotional self-awareness
- self-control or emotional self-regulation
- self-motivation
- empathy
- social skills

To begin with, self-knowledge refers to the knowledge of our feelings and emotions. Understand how they affect us and how much they influence our behavior and our decisions. Identify what our capabilities are and what our weak points are. It's crucial to know where we stand and not demand more or less than that.

I know myself well enough to use these resources or tools, so I don't take my anger or frustration home. In my case, for example, when I have a bad day at work, I know I have to go for a run just after getting home. It is an obligation because I know that will be where I leave my discomfort.

Generally, as soon as I get home, I greet my family, change, and leave. I'm not going away for a long time because I want to be with them. I am not running away from them, but trying to be good for them. I know it will be worse if I stay with them and don't eliminate the negative charge that has me distressed.

Knowing each other implies, sometimes, putting yourself in front of everyone. Prioritize your needs, calm your body's demands, and then get on with life.

On the other hand, emotional self-control allows us to reflect and control our feelings or emotions to avoid being carried away by them.

It consists of knowing how to detect emotional dynamics and which ones are temporary and lasting. It means being aware of what aspects of an emotion we can take advantage of and how we can relate to the environment to take away the power of another that harms us more than it benefits us.

Have a clear reference of what happens when you feel something specific. Physiologically speaking, what happens in your body, and what happens in your mind? Your future behavior will depend on it.

For there to be a reaction, it must first have passed through the filter of emotional self-regulation. In a certain sense, a good part of regulating emotions consists of knowing how to manage our focus of attention.

Also, part of self-control requires being able to anticipate consequences.

To master self-regulation, a language is a useful tool. Find the words, the narrative, and the discursive coherence to express ourselves clearly.

Do not leave loose ends, do not leave anything to the interpretation of others. This way, we let the other know our intentions and feelings. And we give it space so that the emotional intelligence of the other comes into action.

Self-motivation has to be with the construction of adequate emotional intelligence. It also affects our ability to set goals, focus, and maintain the level of concentration that allows us to emphasize the positive things along the way instead of the adversities.

To do this, we must start from a purely optimistic basis. Be positive and take the initiative. No one will start this path for us. It is a moment in which, as human beings, we must act and find those factors that maintain our enthusiasm over time.

There will always be unforeseen events; however, you must overcome these obstacles constructively. Conceive them as part of the learning process, as we have seen happens with a flexible mindset. Thanks to the ability to motivate ourselves, we can leave behind those obstacles that are only based on habit or unjustified fear of what might happen.

Empathy is fundamental for the correct development of the social human being. Interpersonal relationships are based on properly interpreting the signals that others express unconsciously and often emit non-verbally.

Recognizing the other's emotions and feelings is the first

step to understanding and identifying with the people who express them. Empathetic people are those who, in general, have greater skills and competencies related to emotional intelligence.

A good relationship with others is an essential source of our personal happiness and even, in many cases, for good job performance. You have to know how to treat and communicate with those who are nice or close to us. Still, one of the keys to emotional intelligence is to do it with people you don't like.

And it is that this type of intelligence is closely related to verbal intelligence, so that, in part, they overlap each other. This may be because part of the way we experience emotions is mediated by our social relationships and by our way of understanding what others say.

Thus, we go beyond thinking about how others make us feel. Any interaction between human beings takes place in a specific context. Perhaps someone has made a derogatory comment about us because he is envious or simply needs to base his social influence on this behavior.

Emotional intelligence helps us think about the causes that have triggered others to behave as they did. Making us feel a certain way instead of thinking about how we feel and deciding how we will react to what we feel.

INTERACTIVE EXERCISES

A good exercise to optimize your levels of emotional intelligence is to think about the motivations for our past actions.

Take a moment, and think of something you have done. It doesn't matter if it was a long time ago. It doesn't matter if you consider it a good deed or not. What matters is how it made you feel.

Analyze what feelings this fact aroused and what mechanism was turned on inside you. Know these variables in your mind, so you can anticipate the facts.

In sports, which brings us here, knowing yourself gives you a substantial advantage over those who don't. Emotional intelligence will allow you to toughen up in difficult moments. Especially if you play individual sports.

If this is the case, think about the last competition you lost. Focus not on your successes, but on your failures. Make a conscious effort to connect with what you felt at the time, and form a concrete idea of how your emotional state works.

That way, the next time you're in a big game, you'll know what feelings to pay attention to, so you can avoid whatever caused you to lose.

Anxiety? Anger? Frustration? We have already seen how to deal with those feelings. You have in your hands the possibility of incorporating emotional maturity into your sports performance.

At this point, an extra mile is necessary when the structural changes we discussed at the beginning are achieved. Building our emotional intelligence optimizes our chances of success. It can mean a fraction of a second less than our rival.

As a counterpart to anxiety (which could determine our failure), emotional intelligence can become the key tool that allows us to succeed. Through her, we will be able to strengthen our behaviors and move forward.

Next, we will see the importance of mental strength. Another significant factor in the path of high-performance athletes, and through which the vast majority of great sports stars live their lives.

6

YOUR CHANCE TO INSPIRE SOMEONE ELSE

"Nothing is impossible. The word itself says 'I'm possible!'"

— AUDREY HEPBURN

My goal in writing this book is to inspire you to achieve what may seem impossible when you look at it head-on. It's to show you that when your mind, body, and heart are in line with your goals, those things that seem impossible really aren't, and all you have to do to achieve them is get started.

I hope you're already feeling that inspiration, and that, page by page, you're developing the motivation and the mindset you need to succeed, not only in your athletic goals but in any goal you set your mind to.

Inspiration is powerful... and this is your opportunity to pass it on to someone else.

The beauty is that you don't yet have to have completed

your own transformation to inspire someone else to begin theirs… All you have to do is share with them your motivation and the things driving you.

And you can do that right now simply by writing a few sentences.

By leaving a review of this book on Amazon, you can inspire someone else to improve their mental strength and ensure every part of their being is in line with their athletic goals.

How? When you let other readers know how this book has inspired you and what they'll find within its pages, you'll show them where they can find the same inspiration that kickstarted your transformation.

Thank you for helping me on my mission to show everyone that they can achieve their dreams. Inspiration is a powerful tool; when we share it, we can help each other take the steps we need to achieve anything we desire.

7

TOUGH LIKE STEEL

Mental Toughness in Athletes

It is important to overcome the conditioning of our own minds. Some athletes start in their disciplines because they discover they are good at it. They win their first competitions as children and begin believing that winning a competition is innate. Which is part of their personalities.

A child's athletic potential is properly established, both through their victories and defeats. This is not bad per se, as long as it is accompanied (and contained) by the athlete's coach. In this sense, the coach's work involves making the child understand that the road is hard beyond their victories.

Its Importance in Sports

In the case of Mariano Varde (former continental swimmer), his beginnings in swimming were with mixed feelings. At an early age, he discovered he knew how to swim. He found that he was good at what he did. He started setting good times and easily beating his competitors, regardless of the category and style they swam.

However, over the years, he discovered something was wrong with him. He had been practicing his sport for some time, reaping triumphs, growing as an athlete, but only from the image he gave to others. The idea of an outstanding athlete, even from an early age. A swimming prodigy. However, inside him, the reality was very different.

Not only was it difficult for him to find enough motivation (or the necessary one) to conceive this sport as part of his life, but at times, his mental deficits deepened.

He felt like, at times, he wasn't the one doing the swimming. It was not him who jumped into the water, who left that physical and mental effort in his sport. Rather, he felt that he swam for others, for all those who had placed their expectations, projections, and unfulfilled desires on him, a child.

There came a time when the others were motivated and not him. That situation exposed him to levels of anxiety, pressure, and anguish, driving him away from the sport. The objectives, expectations, and wishes of triumph were foreign and did not coincide with what dictated his heart.

From that moment on, Varde dedicated himself to

enjoying his teen years. Enjoying his adolescence away from sports, something that young athletes can rarely do.

At 22, after hitting rock bottom and not finding his way, a voice inside him told him that he should swim again. From that moment on, he incorporated swimming back into his daily life, and he did so by motivating himself in different ways.

First, he decided to take the lifeguard course. Later, when he managed to get into the rhythm of the competition, he regained his place as one of the best swimmers on the continent. Only four months after his return, he was already participating in the national final of his style.

He continued his career by consecrating himself at the national level several times in different styles of swimming, which allowed him to develop his life (sentimental and professional) always next to a pool. However, his mental toughness did not go with him when he had opportunities to climb to continental and world levels.

He recognizes that, at that time, he did not have the emotional intelligence necessary to live with the pressure of sports results determining a job or a scholarship. The possibility of reaching the highest rank of swimmers surpassed him. He felt that anguish again, that pressure, and that weight on his back. And he stopped enjoying competitive swimming.

Mariano was able to understand, apply, and live the importance of mental strength used in sports as an adult when he became coach of the River Plate mayor swimming team.

He used his limitation's transformative power when he could let go of the pressure of his own results and focus on teaching young swimmers how to build successful careers as athletes.

A clear example of the destructive power of poorly channeled sports pressure is that of the Argentine swimmer Delfina Pignatiello. She was running to be one of the best athletes on the continent, and her lack of mental toughness cost her the race. She retired from sports competitions when she was only 22 years old to dedicate herself to photography.

INTERACTIVE EXERCISES

The old proverb *mens sana in corpore sano* (a healthy mind in a healthy body) makes sense when it is understood that health must be sought integrally. The most powerful way to combat anxiety is to constantly work on building your resilience and mental toughness.

Start by analyzing the situations that come your way. Try to relax, think about them calmly, and act on them. It will be necessary to optimize our attention as a tool to facilitate the passage between moments of anxiety.

Therefore, we must redirect toward these good behaviors in our daily lives. Even sensations such as fear can bring back moments in which we have failed and allow us to be more careful.

Try to focus on the good results.

As we discuss in this chapter, mental toughness will be critical to success and should be addressed from a young age. Explain to young athletes the importance of considering failure as part of the learning process in the early stages of training.

We will not be able to ask them to have an adult's emotional maturity or mental integrity. Adult athletes, especially those already established, achieved their goals by working this long and arduous path with sacrifice and perseverance.

If mental strength falters, so will our performance, and, understandably, this situation generates fear in us.

We will see below how to deal with these fears, especially the most common fears for athletes: the fear of failure and the fear of missing out.

8

DEALING WITH YOUR FEARS

Fear of Failure

One of the most dramatic and emotional moments observed during a sports competition is the shooting of a penalty shootout in the final rounds of a competition, such as a soccer world cup.

In this definition, tension is constantly escalating. Sometimes it is possible to see the panic on the faces of some players and even guess who will fail based on the degree of tension reflected in their walk.

These penalty rounds are moments when even the best players in the world are capable of missing their shots. The tension that happens in these moments overwhelms even the sport's superstars.

The fact is that fear is an emotion that has a decisive influence on sports performance. Its effects can be devastating for athletes. Fear can lead a successful and talented athlete to a performance block. Losing, even for a fraction of a second, everything they know.

What Is It?

The athlete is not afraid of failure, but is scared of the consequences of failure. The desire to succeed and be better than others can lead to tension, anxiety, and fear of failure.

Likewise, the main fears of the consequences that the athletes attribute to failure would be their self-esteem, punishment, and the loss of their social value. Therefore, the fear of suffering one of these situations leads the athlete to avoid situations that he conceives as dangerous or decisive.

In this way, the athlete begins to play conditioned. Paying too much attention to not making mistakes and losing focus on other aspects of the game. This is part of an attempted solution that is dysfunctional and counterproductive. The point is that, due to this attempted solution, the athlete falls into their own trap.

Symptoms

If you suffer from fear of failure, you will be able to realize that anxiety will prevent you from being able to carry out a good performance.

Negative stress, which manifests itself due to fear of failure, will result in us not being able to function properly. This is why the fear of failure can lead to considerable psychic suffering.

However, it is important to clearly distinguish between fear and anxiety. Fear is an emotion that activates, in a fraction of a second, certain physiological responses to give a fight or flight response.

When this physical reaction is maintained over time beyond the immediate response, we call it anxiety. Therefore, it is considered a defence mechanism that, in these cases, can have negative consequences.

There are three types of symptoms attributable to fear of failure. Physical, cognitive, and behavioral symptoms.

As for the physical ones, they are similar to those described in the chapter on anxiety. Palpitations, increased heart rate, shortness of breath, and a feeling of being trapped.

Cognitive symptoms concern the perception of fear and its psychological consequences. The fear of failure can generate internal guilt for not meeting a goal and high levels of self-demand. It can seriously blow a person's mood, self-esteem, and confidence.

These symptoms are personal and internal to each athlete, and depending on their emotional intelligence and maturity, they will have greater or lesser psychological and physical consequences.

Finally, behavioral symptoms are those that are evident in dealing with others and in the way the athlete acts. If the subject suffers these fears, he can change his training routines. Reduce his commitment levels, or stop taking care of himself with the necessary meals and exercises. You can also see a change in dealing with their peers and opponents.

How to Overcome It?

This fear of failure can have numerous origins. Maybe because of the individual conception of what failure implies. Also, because of the catastrophic anticipation of what the consequences of failure could be.

So far, we have defined the fear of failure and how common it is. Now, since we have all been through it at some point, we want to tell you strategies to overcome it, to know what to do when we feel it approaching.

Try to be realistic. Try to see how big the risk is, how severe it is, and how likely it is to happen. We assure you that, if you calmly think about all these factors, you will see that nothing was as serious as it seemed.

It's a good idea to start with intermediate goals: not too easy to be a real challenge, but not extremely difficult or impossible. Realistic and challenging goals will generate satisfaction and, at the same time, keep us from the probability of failing.

It is advisable to analyze what part of failing anguishes you, generates fear, and keeps you from trying. Once the fear factor is identified, it will be much easier to work to overcome it and prevent anxiety from taking over us.

Failure is something that could happen. It should not be a cause for extreme distress. We can fail and try again. Adopting this idea is essential if what we seek is to overcome the fear of failure.

Look for techniques that help propel you forward. Establish a goal for which we do something, do things that pleasure us, and, therefore, the desire to continue doing it. It will help us when carrying out a task we see the possibility of failing.

Anxiety leads us to anticipate scenarios that are negative and cause us discomfort. Being realistic, we cannot be certain of what will happen. Avoid imagining possible outcomes, and you will feel much better.

Being self-demanding can be good, but it stops being so when it interferes with our health and well-being. Very high levels of self-demand are extremely harmful.

Fear of Missing Out

FOMO, also known as the fear of missing out, is one of the new health issues of our time. It has been recognized by psychologists as a disorder that can lead to serious emotional and mental problems.

Since social networks burst into our lives, being continuously connected through our mobile phones can cause behavior problems or habits that generate syndromes such as FOMO.

Those suffering from this syndrome are constantly hooked on their mobile or internet-enabled device and fear missing any comments or events. We are talking about those people who, when they are with their mobile phone, go through all the social networks they use one by one, and as soon as they finish their journey, they start all over again to see if they missed anything in the last few minutes. Also, those people who are constantly touching the refresh button.

Thus, they need to know their followers and what they are doing. They also believe that, if they don't answer them immediately, they will miss important things and be left out of the conversation. And this idea already causes them anguish, so it will be difficult for them to disconnect or put aside their phone. In this way, FOMO is intimately linked with the irrational fear of not having your cell phone.

Among the symptoms of FOMO stands out the syndrome of the phantom call or alert, which refers to the illusory sounds that one thinks one hears from the mobile, such as the auditory notification of a message. Our brain gets so used to the use of the mobile that it incorporates it in such a way into daily life that it deceives us with this type of thing. For its part, there is also the anxiety caused by not responding to a message or a comment immediately on any social network.

Another symptom is the sufferer's excessive time on social networks, such as Facebook, TikTok, Instagram, Twitter, or WhatsApp. Constantly broadcasting what they are doing, where they are, what they have been wearing, etc.

This is combined with taking pictures, recording videos, and forgetting to live in the moment. So much so that they are constantly looking at the screen during family reunions, vacations, concerts, and working hours.

Because the difference is there: it is not a punctual behavior throughout the day, but continuous from morning to night. This type of behavior can be observed in people

Dealing With Your Fears

who forget to use their eyes when taking a video of an event. They do not physically connect with what is happening, but only through their phone screen.

This way of acting usually results in reproaches from the environment to put the phone aside. That is why the person is moody and irritable and prefers to stay alone or isolate themselves in their room rather than separate from the network and miss something.

Studies have proven that most people who suffer from this syndrome are young people who constantly need to be accepted by a group. They also need to feel loved and flattered, and often compete with the rest of their lives on social networks to feel equal. Or better.

In fact, FOMO causes a cognitive distortion by which reality is not appreciated. The critical vision of what is fiction or a relative fact is lost in a much broader context that we do not know, the one that appears on the screen.

But young people are not the only ones to suffer from this problem, and it is contrary to what one might think. Those who suffer the most from FOMO are people of any age with a low level of satisfaction in their life and very low self-esteem.

They have a tendency to maintain dependency relationships. They must receive likes, compliments, and positive comments to love themselves. They escape through the network from a reality with which they are unsatisfied.

The solution to this problem is to first address the cause that has caused it. FOMO can cause anxiety and depression and further increase self-esteem problems and frustrations that lead to behavioral disorders.

Leaving social networks or throwing away your mobile phone will not solve anything, since all you can do is avoid the problem. Let's recognize that networks are part of our lives and that, even if it's just for work, most need to use them.

It is necessary to change mobile use habits and adopt appropriate behavior. Be rational in network management, take care of your self-esteem, and focus your efforts daily to find a balance in their use.

Educate by example and remember that human contact, which allows us to know the expressions and emotions of the other without saying a word, is essential for the development of children and young people. They will hardly be able to learn empathy if they often interact through screens. Sometimes even when they are physically in the same room or on the same street.

However, suppose you have discovered that you suffer from FOMO. In that case, it is best to seek help from a professional psychologist, who will guide you and give you the necessary tools to overcome and properly manage this problem.

INTERACTIVE EXERCISES

You cannot make fear the factor that governs and controls your life, and for this, we will give you the best ways and tips to work on fear through psychotherapy:

Write your fears on paper: This is a very simple activity. It consists of scribbling and writing on a sheet of paper what causes you anxiety.

On the left side, write words, pictures, or phrases about things that make you feel bad or fear. On the right side, write, doodle, or draw everything that gives you a feeling of comfort and then make a comparison between the two. When you discover that what is on the right side gives you peace of mind, you can safely face them.

Create mental protection: A simple way to feel safe and fearless is to create mental safety around you; when you face your fear, close your eyes, and imagine that you are inside a bubble or in a quiet and peaceful place. Cozy, where you cannot be reached by your fear. That way, you won't be afraid to approach it.

Rationalize your fear: fears are irrational, so giving them a logic will help you analyze and understand them: Why are you afraid? Why does it happen? Is it as bad as it seems? Does it have power over you? When you ask yourself these questions and answer them, it will allow you to reduce the level that fear influences you.

According to what has been seen in this chapter, amateur and professional athletes must deal with different fears throughout their careers. These fears and concerns can be paralyzing, negatively affecting your performance.

To do this, it is first necessary to recognize them as such and act on it. Take them as a natural part of the learning process, and try not to panic.

The proper treatment of these fears will be a fundamental factor to cope with difficult times, with determination and a positive mentality. In this way we can minimize the chances that, for this reason, we will make mistakes typical of this problem.

We will see in the next chapter, what these common mistakes are, that many athletes commit due to fear and insecurities.

9
COMMON MISTAKES ATHLETES MAKE

When an athlete is not mentally able to maintain their level, they often make decisions that, over the years, are proven wrong. And this type of behavior occurs in any kind of athlete: amateur, semi-amateur, or professional. Even some of the greatest athletes in history, such as the case we see below.

Michael Jordan had just been an Olympic champion with the unrepeatable United States Dream Team in 1992. He led the Chicago Bulls to their first three-time NBA championship a year later. By the mid-1990s, he was the leading figure in basketball worldwide.

His playing excellence, combined with his overall winner mentality beginning to take shape and size, had him at the center of the stage, not only within the league but in the world of sports. His Majesty was a mass phenomenon on the planet, someone completely transcended.

But, suddenly, Michael Jordan retired from the NBA and went to try his luck in professional baseball.

His first retirement was announced in 1993. The reasons? There are several theories about it, but it is believed it had to do with the murder of his father at 56.

This event marked him forever and is believed to be decisive for MJ's next steps. The pain of his departure was devastating for the athlete.

The concrete thing is that Jordan Sr. was a lover of baseball, which Michael had practiced as a child. And part of that paternal taste for the sport led the Bulls's star to try his luck in another field.

Steve Kerr recognized in The Jump that:

Michael faced all kinds of public scrutiny. I will always maintain that he went to play baseball because he was emotionally burned by that scrutiny that only he really felt. Seeing the life he had to wear compared to the rest was crazy. I think he had had enough and needed to run for a while. When he returned, he was ready to continue.

For Jordan, of course, it was not a simple game to pass the time. He got fully involved in the dynamics of the team, he trained to improve himself, and he lived with the criticism of the specialized press of the time. Like everything in his life, he put passion, hard work, and a quest to compete and improve himself to show that he was up to the task.

Jordan did something crazy: he was not out of tune at all, considering the abrupt and sudden change from a discipline that he dominated to another that he had never tried in that field and context.

He finished his short baseball career with a .202 batting average, which is not the best in the cold. Still, the situation went far beyond the statistics of the game, and he moved to the stands. In that season, the Barons set their home crowd record: nearly half a million viewers.

Newbies Blunders

Until a young athlete acquires a certain degree of knowledge of the details of their discipline, they spend time where, most likely, they will make mistakes due to their inexperience.

You see, in all sports and categories, there are young athletes who have all the necessary conditions to succeed and who eventually do, but not without first making some of these mistakes that we mentioned.

They are common and are a natural part of the learning process. In addition, as we will see, even the greatest athletes on the planet (consecrated and with their entire career resolved) are also wrong.

To minimize the chances of making mistakes, the young athlete must consider some key aspects, including adequate training and the correct interpretation of how to grow as a sports professional.

However, it is essential to emphasize that to err is human. It will depend on the character of the athlete and the approach that their coach chooses so that this premise is always on the table.

Sometimes, some young athletes do not give themselves

totally to training. Either because they do not perform the previous warm-up properly or they do not dedicate the necessary time to the aerobic aspect.

Even a problem for young athletes is balancing their social lives with competitions.

Veteran Blunders

With the passing of the years and the athletic career of an athlete, the physiological aspects (logically) are altered. Performance declines, and the time needed to physically recover increases with age.

Some expert athletes fight against this as if it were possible to modify an inescapable reality: the passage of time and physical and mental deterioration is inevitable.

Some common mistakes older athletes make are, for example, related to the difference between bodily and mental age. Many of them, internally, still feel young and believe they have the physical capacity to respond to the demands of the game. However, the heart does not beat as before, and the muscle mass is not the same, which can lead to serious injuries.

Adapting training and physical demands to a condition, context, and age is essential. For this, they must learn to listen to their bodies. Be aware when you feel tired or when the physical forces you to rest.

High-intensity training is the key. It prepares the body well for hard work by developing a good base. However, intensity also brings tiredness, fatigue, and an increased risk of injury.

The muscles do not recover as before. This means taking more time between quality sessions and being very focused on recovery strategies.

AFTERWORD

Throughout the book, we have gone through different strategies to positively channel the anxieties in sports. As athletes, we know that pressures, fears, and insecurities (our own and others') can have a negative effect on our performance.

The idea of this reading is that, through the correct channeling of these variables, the athlete's performance can be maintained at the levels necessary to succeed in whatever discipline they practice.

For this, we have seen that it is necessary to follow some specific steps correlative between them and where, if one is missing, the other may not come true. For example, the first and most important thing will be the mentality with which we face the practice of any sport.

When we talk about practice, we refer to everything the discipline implies. The training, the mental preparation, the previous study of the rivals, and the variables within the game. In addition, we get ready to be able to perform at our best.

Being optimistic, positive, and flexible will be essential to start the path correctly. Maintain a receptive position regarding the learning process, deal with the constructive opinions of others, and also become our most ardent critics.

Begin by understanding that our mindset sets the pace for everything else. Through it, we can correctly deal with the anxiety generated by sports.

Building a good level of self-esteem and knowledge and being the architects of our own destiny, and minimizing everything that does not depend on us and that we cannot control are some of the benefits of incorporating a winning mentality.

Also, through this achievement, we will understand that failing is part of the game. Removing pressure from the error will be of great help. Because in those cases, when the error arrives (and believe me, it will come), we will be able to deal with it without major inconveniences.

We have also seen that the error is not always ours. Sometimes it's a teammate's or the coach's, even when it's not mistakes that come along the way but unforeseen events or adversities. And life is what happens between one unexpected event and the next.

For this, the power of our mind is essential. Our body will always follow it, consciously or unconsciously, wherever the mind goes. Control the visualization of our goals and objectives, always thinking of positive scenarios to build the necessary strength to cope with those moments. This book

Afterword

tries to teach us to identify sports anxiety and emotional differences.

Recognize the moments in which that enthusiasm typical of sport can turn into anxiety. Anxiety can lead to fears and behaviors that do not favor us. Believing in your abilities and talents should not be an act of faith. Believing in yourself must respond to the support of facts and evidence, like everything in this life.

Words are light; they fly with the wind. The facts, however, the behaviors one adopts, the concrete decisions, mark the subject. In a sports competition, they can be decisive.

Being well mentally, being at peace with oneself, is an essential part of all this. It's a great factor in gaining an edge over your rivals, who are probably just as talented, dedicated, committed, and successful as you are.

Once this initial process is completed, and you have these variables in the order in your life, the next stage of the sports career begins. It is the stage in which you reap achievements and victories through your effort and sacrifice.

During this period, the power of emotional intelligence comes into play. Through the strength of your mind and heart, you will be able to deal with all factors smoothly. Training sessions will be learning moments built from enjoyment. The victories will be the icing on the cake. The finishing touch of the entire previous process.

The defeats will be to reflect and learn from them and understand them as natural and expected events typical of all sports. Getting to this point won't be easy, I'm telling you.

If you're reading this, chances are you're already familiar with some of the strategies described in the book. Perhaps some are completely new, or you know them by ear but have never tried them. I invite you to retrace this path of personal and professional growth with an open mind and a willing heart. To walk this path, be aware that it will be challenging and that it will test all our qualities and our deepest fears.

Do it for yourself, for your goals, and objectives. Do it accompanied, surrounded by positive people. Set an example for your peers, inspire them to excel, and pay particular attention to the training you receive from your coaches. The result will be positive with all this psychological structure put together and applied to your sport and your life. Always, without exceptions.

As always in life, there will be happy and sad moments. Great victories and devastating defeats. But if you keep your enthusiasm, motivation, a clear goal, love, and you accept and know yourself, you can't fail. Go ahead and go for it!

10

TIME TO PASS THE BATON

As you align your mindset with the goals, you want to achieve and harness its powers to get around all the challenges that your sport presents, you put yourself in an excellent position to inspire someone else.

SIMPLY BY LEAVING your honest opinion of this book on Amazon, you'll show new readers where they can find all the tools they need to excel in their sport and meet any goal they set their mind to.

Thank you so much for spreading the word. You can overcome whatever challenge lies in your way – and you can inspire someone else to do the same.

>>> Click here to leave your review on Amazon.

Or scan this QR

BIBLIOGRAPHY

3 Essential Mindsets for Athletic Success. (n.d.). Psychology Today. https://www.psychologytoday.com/us/blog/the-power-prime/201411/3-essential-mindsets-athletic-success

5 Tips to Mental Toughness in Sports. (2021, July 1). Www.donovanmentalperformance.com. https://www.donovanmentalperformance.com/5-tips-to-mental-toughness-in-sports

6 Fears That Destroy Confidence | Sports Psychology Articles. (2013, October 29). https://www.peaksports.com/sports-psychology-blog/6-fears-that-destroy-confidence-for-athletes/

7 most common training mistakes by masters athletes. (2018, March 27). Pan Pacific Masters Games. https://mastersgames.com.au/ppmg/7-most-common-training-mistakes-by-masters-athletes/

7 Strategies to Help You Become a Mentally Strong Runner During Races. (2014, January 6). Runners Connect. https://runnersconnect.net/visualization-running/

10 Simple Exercises to Help Build Your Mental Toughness. (n.d.). Fatherly. Retrieved September 17, 2022, from https://www.fatherly.com/love-money/mental-toughness-exercises

Arlin Cuncic. (2008a, February 22). *Coping With Pre-Competition Nervousness.* Verywell Mind; Verywellmind. https://www.verywellmind.com/coping-with-precompetition-anxiety-in-athletes-3024338

Arlin Cuncic. (2008b, February 22). *How To Handle Performance Anxiety as an Athlete.* Verywell Mind; Verywellmind. https://www.verywellmind.com/how-do-i-handle-performance-anxiety-as-an-athlete-3024337

Barker, E. (2016, June 7). *This Is The Best Way to Overcome Fear of Missing Out.* Time; Time. https://time.com/4358140/overcome-fomo/

Bettin, A. (2017, October 3). *Avoiding Mental Sabotage Part 6: How to Conquer Your Fear of Failure.* TrainingPeaks. https://www.trainingpeaks.com/blog/avoiding-mental-sabotage-part-6-how-to-conquer-your-fear-of-failure/

Can You Get Stronger By Just Thinking About it? (n.d.). Verywell Fit.

Bibliography

https://www.verywellfit.com/can-you-build-strength-with-visualization-exercises-3120698

Carol Dweck. (2022, April 20). Wikipedia. https://es.wikipedia.org/wiki/Carol_Dweck

Cherry, K. (2010, April 27). *6 Key Ideas Behind Theories of Motivation.* Verywell Mind; Verywellmind. https://www.verywellmind.com/theories-of-motivation-2795720

Cherry, K. (2021, April 29). *Why Cultivating a Growth Mindset Can Boost Your Success.* Verywell Mind. https://www.verywellmind.com/what-is-a-mindset-2795025

Cherry, K. (2022, August 3). *Overview of emotional intelligence.* Verywell Mind. https://www.verywellmind.com/what-is-emotional-intelligence-2795423

Competition performance: five techniques to help you control anxiety. (2017, February 17). Sports Performance Bulletin. https://www.sportsperformancebulletin.com/endurance-psychology/coping-with-emotions/sports-anxiety-theory-research/

Davidson, A. (2019). *3 Types of Psychological Stress Affecting Athletes In-season - Firstbeat Sports.* Firstbeat. https://www.firstbeat.com/en/blog/3-types-of-psychological-stress-affecting-athletes-in-season/

Does Pressure Affect Performance? | Sports Psychology Articles. (2019). Peaksports.com. https://www.peaksports.com/sports-psychology-blog/does-pressure-affect-your-performance-during-competitions/

Elizabeth Scott. (2021, April 25). *Do You Have FOMO? Here Is How to Cope.* Verywell Mind. https://www.verywellmind.com/how-to-cope-with-fomo-4174664

Emotional Intelligence for Sports Coaches & Athletes | RocheMartin. (n.d.). Www.rochemartin.com. Retrieved September 17, 2022, from https://www.rochemartin.com/emotional-intelligence-sports

Emotional intelligence in sports: The game within the game - BelievePerform - The UK's leading Sports Psychology Website. (2013, May 24). BelievePerform - the UK's Leading Sports Psychology Website. https://believeperform.com/emotional-intelligence-in-sports-the-game-within-the-game/

EndurElite. (n.d.). *5 Powerful Exercises for Increasing Your Competitive Confidence.* EndurElite. Retrieved September 17, 2022, from https://endurelite.com/blogs/free-nutrition-supplement-and-training-articles-for-runners-and-cyclists/5-powerful-exercises-for-increasing-your-competitive-confidence

Fear of Failure (Atychiphobia): Causes & Treatment. (n.d.). Cleveland Clinic.

https://my.clevelandclinic.org/health/diseases/22555-atychiphobia-fear-of-failure

Fear of Failure: Causes & 5 Ways to Cope with Atychiphobia. (n.d.). Choosing Therapy. https://www.choosingtherapy.com/fear-of-failure/

Fixed versus growth intelligence mindsets: It's all in your head, Dweck says | Stanford News Release. (2007, February 7). Stanford.edu. https://news.stanford.edu/pr/2007/pr-dweck-020707.html

Ford, J., Ildefonso, K., Jones, M., & Arvinen-Barrow, M. (2017). *Sport-related anxiety: current insights.* Open Access Journal of Sports Medicine, Volume 8(1), 205–212. https://doi.org/10.2147/oajsm.s125845

Forrester, N. W. (2019, February 22). *How Olympians train their brains to become mentally tough.* The Conversation. https://theconversation.com/how-olympians-train-their-brains-to-become-mentally-tough-92110

Frollo, J. (n.d.). *7 mistakes many athletes don't recognize until they get older.* Blogs.usafootball.com. https://blogs.usafootball.com/blog/694/7-mistakes-many-athletes-don-t-recognize-until-they-get-older

Giandonato, J. (2022, February 10). *The 6 Worst Mistakes Football Players Make in the Off-Season.* Stack. https://www.stack.com/a/off-season-football-mistakes/

Godwin, R. (2019, April 7). *Age is no barrier: meet the world's oldest top athletes.* The Guardian; The Guardian. https://www.theguardian.com/global/2019/apr/07/age-is-no-barrier-meet-the-oldest-top-athletes

Gupta, S., & Mccarthy, P. (n.d.). *Sporting resilience during CoVid-19: What is the nature of this adversity and how are competitive-elite athletes adapting?* https://doi.org/10.3389/fpsyg.2021.611261

Haden, J. (2014, July 23). *7 Habits of People With Remarkable Mental Toughness.* Inc.com. https://www.inc.com/jeff-haden/7-habits-of-people-with-remarkable-mental-toughness.html

Hamilton, A. (2017, February 17). *Sports psychology: self-confidence in sport – make your ego work for you!* Sports Performance Bulletin. https://www.sportsperformancebulletin.com/endurance-psychology/coping-with-emotions/sports-psychology-self-confidence-sport-make-ego-work/

Happy Anxiety: Feeling Anxious About Things You're Excited About. (2019, October 7). Healthline. https://www.healthline.com/health/i-feel-anxious-about-things-i-enjoy#1

How To Cope With Sport Performance Anxiety - Tips And Advice. (2021, July 14). Forth Edge. https://www.forthedge.co.uk/knowledge/how-to-cope-with-sport-performance-anxiety/

Bibliography

How to do visualization effectively for sports. (2014, December 23). Mental Toughness Trainer. https://www.mentaltoughnesstrainer.com/visualization-techniques-for-sports/

How to Overcome Fear of Failure | Indeed.com. (2019). Indeed.com. https://www.indeed.com/career-advice/career-development/how-to-overcome-fear-of-failure

https://www.facebook.com/jamesclear, & Clear, J. (2013, April 11). *The Science of Developing Mental Toughness in Health, Work, and Life*. James Clear. https://jamesclear.com/mental-toughness

InnerDrive. (n.d.). *9 Ways Olympians Develop Resilience*. Blog.innerdrive.co.uk. https://blog.innerdrive.co.uk/9-ways-olympians-develop-resilience

Institute for Health and Human Potential. (2019). *What Is Emotional Intelligence, Daniel Goleman*. IHHP. https://www.ihhp.com/meaning-of-emotional-intelligence/

Kopp, A., & Jekauc, D. (2018). *The Influence of Emotional Intelligence on Performance in Competitive Sports: A Meta-Analytical Investigation*. Sports, 6(4), 175. https://doi.org/10.3390/sports6040175

Lawton, J. (2021, June 22). *Managing Athlete FOMO*. TrainingPeaks. https://www.trainingpeaks.com/coach-blog/managing-athlete-fomo/

Loder, V. (n.d.). *How To Conquer The Fear Of Failure - 5 Proven Strategies*. Forbes. Retrieved September 17, 2022, from https://www.forbes.com/sites/vanessaloder/2014/10/30/how-to-move-beyond-the-fear-of-failure-5-proven-strategies/?sh=7f09012e1b78

Mahaffey, D. (n.d.). Council Post: *Five Ways To Develop A Winning Mindset*. Forbes. Retrieved September 17, 2022, from https://www.forbes.com/sites/forbescoachescouncil/2017/09/22/five-ways-to-develop-a-winning-mindset/?sh=e5a00444ca2a

Mariama-Arthur, K. (2016, January 25). *Why Every Leader Needs Mental Toughness*. Entrepreneur. https://www.entrepreneur.com/leadership/why-every-leader-needs-mental-toughness/250989

Mariama-Arthur, K. (2017, February 24). *Why Mindset Mastery Is Vital to Your Success*. Entrepreneur. https://www.entrepreneur.com/leadership/why-mindset-mastery-is-vital-to-your-success/285466

Mental Edge: Fear is an athlete's worst enemy. (2019, January 31). USA TODAY High School Sports. https://usatodayhss.com/2019/mental-edge-fear-is-an-athletes-worst-enemy

Mental Toughness Training for Athletes. (2016, March 17). Mental Toughness

Bibliography

Training for Athletes. Sports Psychology Articles. https://www.peaksports.com/sports-psychology-blog/mental-toughness-training-athletes/

Metrifit. (2020, March 5). *Self Confidence and Performance. Metrifit Ready to Perform.* https://metrifit.com/blog/good-preparation-breeds-confidence/

Milani, J. (2019, April 4). *The Power of Mindset on Sports Performance.* Www.sportsmd.com. https://www.sportsmd.com/2019/04/04/the-power-of-mindset-on-sports-performance/

Mind Tools Content Team. (2009). *Overcoming Fear of FailureFacing Fears and Moving Forward.* Mindtools.com. https://www.mindtools.com/pages/article/fear-of-failure.htm

Mindset: ¿Qué es y para qué sirve? (n.d.). Https://Www.crehana.com. Retrieved September 17, 2022, from https://www.crehana.com/blog/negocios/mindset/

Morin, A. (2019, November 21). *10 Exercises That Will Help You Develop the Mental Strength You Need to Crush Your Goals.* Inc.com. https://www.inc.com/amy-morin/10-exercises-that-will-help-you-develop-mental-strength-you-need-to-cr.html

Olympians Use Imagery as Mental Training. (2014, February 22). The New York Times. https://www.nytimes.com/2014/02/23/sports/olympics/olympians-use-imagery-as-mental-training.html

Peppercorn, S. (2018, December 10). *How to Overcome Your Fear of Failure.* Harvard Business Review. https://hbr.org/2018/12/how-to-overcome-your-fear-of-failure

Prabhu, U. (2022, June 25). *Where the Head goes; Body follows.* Medium. https://medium.com/@urmilastories503/where-the-head-goes-body-follows-2c50d7de6562

Quinn, E. (2018). *Visualization and mental rehearsal can improve athletic performance.* Verywell Fit. https://www.verywellfit.com/visualization-techniques-for-athletes-3119438

Quinn, E. (2021, June 11). *How Keeping a Positive Attitude Can Improve Sports Performance.* Verywell Fit. https://www.verywellfit.com/attitude-and-sports-performance-3974677

Resilience and Overcoming Performance Errors | Sports Psychology Today - Sports Psychology. (2014, July 11). Www.sportpsychologytoday.com. https://www.sportpsychologytoday.com/sport-psychology-for-athletes/resilience-and-overcoming-performance-errors/

Rice, S. M., Gwyther, K., Santesteban-Echarri, O., Baron, D., Gorczynski, P., Gouttebarge, V., Reardon, C. L., Hitchcock, M. E., Hainline, B., & Purcell,

Bibliography

R. (2019). *Determinants of anxiety in elite athletes: a systematic review and meta-analysis.* British Journal of Sports Medicine, 53(11), 722–730. https://doi.org/10.1136/bjsports-2019-100620

Rodriguez-Romo, G., Blanco-Garcia, C., Diez-Vega, I., & Acebes-Sánchez, J. (2021). *Emotional Intelligence of Undergraduate Athletes: The Role of Sports Experience.* Frontiers in Psychology, 12. https://doi.org/10.3389/fpsyg.2021.609154

Rovello, J. (2016, August 23). *5 Ways Katie Ledecky, Michael Phelps, and Other Olympians Visualize Success.* Inc.com. https://www.inc.com/jessica-rovello/five-steps-to-visualize-success-like-an-olympian.html

S.L, S. C. A., & Coordinador. (2021, April 11). *How to respond to athletes' mistakes.* SportCoach. https://sportcoach.es/en/how-to-respond-to-athletes-mistakes/

Sager, J. (2022, December 29). *100 inspirational quotes to keep you inspired in 2022 —You can do hard things! Parade: Entertainment, Recipes, Health, Life, Holidays.* https://parade.com/973277/jessicasager/inspirational-quotes/

Segal, J., Smith, M., Robinson, L., & Shubin, J. (2019). *Improving Emotional Intelligence (EQ).* HelpGuide.org. https://www.helpguide.org/articles/mental-health/emotional-intelligence-eq.htm

Self Confidence. (n.d.). Www.brianmac.co.uk. https://www.brianmac.co.uk/selfcon.htm

src="https://secure.gravatar.com/avatar/7bb80e48b9bcb1a4b267e5bc973ed817?s=96, img class="avatar" alt="Steve M., #038;d=mm, Jun. 23, 038;r=g" width="50" height="50">Steve M., & 2022. (n.d.). *10 Worst Mistakes in Sports History.* Reader's Digest. Retrieved September 17, 2022, from https://www.rd.com/list/5-worst-mistakes-in-sports-history/

Swaim, E. (2022, March 9). *Why Sports Anxiety Happens and How to Cope.* Healthline. https://www.healthline.com/health/sports-performance-anxiety

Tank, A. (2019, September 6). *How to learn to embrace your anxiety (and turn it into excitement).* Fast Company. https://www.fastcompany.com/90399444/how-to-learn-to-embrace-your-anxiety-and-turn-it-into-excitement

The Fine Line Between Anxiety and Excitement. (n.d.). Thriveglobal.com. https://thriveglobal.com/stories/the-fine-line-between-anxiety-and-excitement/

The Fine Line Between Fear and Excitement — And How to Cross It. (n.d.).

Bibliography

Www.linkedin.com. https://www.linkedin.com/pulse/fine-line-between-fear-excitement-how-cross-dani-hao/

The Top 10 - The Biggest Mistakes Endurance Athletes Make. (n.d.). Hammer Nutrition. Retrieved September 17, 2022, from https://hammernutrition.com/blogs/essential-knowledge/10-biggest-mistakes-endurance-athletes-make?_pos=1&_psq=10+biggest&_ss=e&_v=1.0

Top 7 Tips: Beginners Visualization Techniques. (2019, August 21). EnVision. https://envision.app/2019/08/21/top-7-beginner-tips-visualization-techniques/

Vallabhjee, S. (2020, August 5). *How Athletes Can Conquer Sports Performance Anxiety.* I Am Herbalife Nutrition – Achieve Inspiring Results. https://iamherbalifenutrition.com/fitness/sports-performance-anxiety/

Vickers, E. (2014, April 28). *Pressure in sport: How real is it?* - Believe Perform - The UK's leading Sports Psychology Website. Believe Perform - the UK's Leading Sports Psychology Website. https://believeperform.com/pressure-in-sport-how-real-is-it/

Visualization and Guided Imagery Techniques for Stress Reduction. (2015). Mentalhelp.net. https://www.mentalhelp.net/stress/visualization-and-guided-imagery-techniques-for-stress-reduction/

West, C. (2018, November 4). *Emotional Intelligence in Sports: How Does it Help...* Exploring Your Mind; Exploring your mind. https://exploringyourmind.com/emotional-intelligence-in-sports-help-you/

What is Mental Toughness? (n.d.). Www.mentaltoughness.partners. https://www.mentaltoughness.partners/what-is-mental-toughness/

Whitener, S. (n.d.). Council *Post: Anxiety Vs. Relaxation: Relabeling Anxiety As Excitement.* Forbes. Retrieved September 17, 2022, from https://www.forbes.com/sites/forbescoachescouncil/2021/04/07/anxiety-vs-relaxation-relabeling-anxiety-as-excitement/?sh=123f304c7afd

Why Fear of Failure Leads to Tentative Play. (2010, April 28). Why Fear of Failure Leads to Tentative Play. Sports Psychology Articles. https://www.peaksports.com/sports-psychology-blog/why-fear-of-failure-leads-to-tentative-play/

Willis, Z. (2019, October 9). *Kevin Love and 6 Other Athletes Who Struggle With Anxiety.* Sportscasting | Pure Sports. https://www.sportscasting.com/kevin-love-and-6-other-athletes-whove-struggled-with-anxiety/

Winning Mentality: 10 Secrets To Developing & Maintaining It. (2021, September 28). Wealthfulmind.com. https://wealthfulmind.com/winning-mentality-secrets-to-developing-it/

Printed in France by Amazon
Brétigny-sur-Orge, FR

14303714R00082